On the Road
Again

On the Road
Again

Travel, Love, and Marriage

**William Hendricks
and
Jim Coté**

**Foreword by Norman Miller
Chairman, Interstate Batteries**

Fleming H. Revell
A Division of Baker Book House
Grand Rapids, Michigan 49516

© 1998 by Front Line Outreach

Published by Fleming H. Revell
a division of Baker Book House Company
P.O. Box 6287, Grand Rapids, MI 49516-6287

Second printing, July 1998

Printed in the United States of America

Library of Congress Cataloging-in-Publication Data

Hendricks, William, 1954–
    On the road again : travel, love, and marriage / William D. Hendricks and Jim Coté ; foreword by Norman Miller.
        p.   cm.
    ISBN 0-8007-5649-5 (paper)
    1. Marriage—United States. 2. Business travel—United States. 3. Married people—Employment—United States. 4. Travelers—United States—Family relationships. 5. Communication in marriage—United States. 6. Separation (Psychology)—United States. I. Coté, Jim. II. Title.
HQ734.H483   1998
306.81—dc21   97-38083

The diagram on page 91 is reprinted from *The Pillars of Marriage* by Norm Wright, copyright 1979, Regal Books, Ventura, CA 93003. Used by permission.

For current information about all releases from Baker Book House, visit our web site:
http://www.bakerbooks.com

Contents

Foreword

No matter how you slice it, business travel—and hence time away from family—will always be necessary for many of us in the workplace today. I really have found no way around it. What is the solution? Not denial, or compromise, or just going ahead and hoping that everything will somehow work out. Instead, after years of business time away from home, I've found that there is actually a way to enhance my family relationships despite the fact that I travel, and that, consequently, those enhanced family relationships enable me to perform better on the road. In other words, I've found a way to make each benefit the other!

The following pages are dedicated to the proposition that business travel does not have to disrupt the stability of your family life or endanger the strength of your marriage—marriage and business travel can actually augment each other, bringing greater fulfillment and satisfaction to your life. Who wouldn't want that?

I've had the privilege of being involved with Interstate Batteries for more than thirty-five years. During that time, I've seen us move from a relatively small, regionally based operation to the largest replacement battery distribution system in North America. I've had the experience of moving from an individual distributor manning a route truck to president and chairman of the board.

Throughout those years, I traveled a lot—a whole lot! Some would say, too much. A lot of things occurred that hurt my family and jeopardized my marriage. But by the grace of God my wife, Anne, and I have been able to overcome those things, and through the process of reviewing my life, taking a hard look at some of my mistakes, and seeking a better way to do business and family, I've discovered some universal principles and truths that have helped me and those associated with me.

The real change began with a decision that would forever influence every aspect of my life: who I am, what I think about, what I say, and what I do. You see, in 1974 I became a Christian. I won't take the time now to delve into all the circumstances that led to that pivotal experience. Suffice it to say that when I became a Christian, my life changed so radically that I began to think about the impact my faith should have on the job. As a result, I became concerned about the family life of our company's national salesmen, who must travel twenty to twenty-five weeks a year.

I could remember only too well my own days on the road, away from Anne and the children, so I had a little perspective on what might be going on in the marriages of some of those salesmen. I wanted to develop a means of encouraging them—to give them some tools to enhance their marriages, even with the separation of travel.

I called a meeting with Jim Coté, our corporate chaplain, and asked him to come up with some materials that would be helpful in addressing marriage and family issues as they relate to salespeople on the road. He called Bill Hendricks, a communications and media production consultant who was familiar with marriage and business issues. Bill had access to a variety of data banks. But after a lengthy search, he couldn't find anything—books, audiotapes, or videocassettes—that related to marriage and traveling salespeople.

So Bill and Jim got together and decided we should produce a video program for this group. The salesmen and their spouses were contacted and asked to name the core issues they struggled with in their marriages. Then, at an Interstate Batteries picnic, Jim casually began to ask a few couples some open-ended questions about their feelings regarding travel-related stress. Within fifteen minutes, he had created a near riot! A crowd gathered, and everyone wanted to get in on the act. We knew we had hit a nerve!

Bill identified the issues that were raised repeatedly in preliminary questioning, and we settled on a dozen topics. We decided on a format in which Jim would interview couples and Dr. Howard G. and Jeanne Hendricks (Bill's parents) would respond to what the couples revealed. Howard and Jeanne are noted authors and worldwide speakers on marriage and family issues.

When the twelve videos were finished, we felt we had a blockbuster (no pun intended), and time has proved us correct. Companion study materials were developed so that each couple would have homework—some exercises to be done together when the salesperson is home, others to be done individually when the person is in the field.

Creating these *Marriage and the Road* videos and study booklets has communicated to our field families how strongly Interstate supports them in the home. We know God was leading us in this project all the way.

We've had requests from other companies and ministries for the *Marriage and the Road* series, and we're pleased with its expanded use. In fact, the success of the series has gone beyond our expectations. We kept hearing, "What's next?" There was no way we could do an encore for this project, but Jim did come up with the idea of a monthly newsletter with the same title. It too has become enormously successful.

Now, after seven years of using videotapes and newsletters to help couples who are hurting, it has dawned on us that we ought to offer this fabulous marriage material to other business travelers. So Bill and Jim have applied their experience and talents to present *Marriage and the Road* in book format. They have spent countless hours discussing, praying about, writing, and revising the information that follows, and I know you're going to like it.

The pages of this book reflect the focus of two men who have studied this subject extensively, with an eye toward practical application of the principles they discovered. Moreover, the insights revealed in these chapters are taken straight from the lives of dozens of business travelers, both inside and outside the Interstate Batteries family.

Jim and Bill's experience and their hours of research have rewarded us all with a wealth of wisdom informed by universal principles—principles that will benefit your marriage. I guarantee that the time you take to read *On the Road Again* will result in clearer insight into your marriage and travel lifestyle, and provide practical advice that will enrich your relationship with your spouse. I hope you enjoy the trip.

Thanks for your investment in your marriage. May God bless you for it!

—Norman Miller

1

Trouble with Travel?
Just Ask Your Family!

*J*im Coté couldn't believe what was happening. The corporate chaplain for Interstate Batteries had been chatting with a group of women at the annual company picnic while their husbands played softball nearby. Many of the men were members of the Interstate sales force, and Jim thought their wives would be a good source of information for a project he was working on. "How do you feel about your husbands being out of town every other week?" he had asked them.

What ensued was a near riot! Women began throwing out comments faster than Jim could absorb them. Some said one thing, others something else. Before long, a sizeable crowd had formed as people began breaking away from the softball field to see what was going on. Once they found out, many were eager to jump into this lively discussion.

The issues they raised were nothing out of the ordinary: finances, communication, parenting, and so on. But the emotion behind their comments was unmistakable. Jim's simple question had struck a raw nerve for the wives of Interstate's "road warriors"—and for the travelers themselves, who quickly chimed in with their own version of how travel was affecting them and their families.

As the intensity of the comments escalated, Jim realized that the only wise thing to do would be to call a halt to the discussion and start over again later in another setting—one more conducive to constructive dialogue and to capturing everyone's insights and emotions.

Marriage and the Road

In this way, a fuse was lit, and *Marriage and the Road*—a unique program that Interstate provides as a company benefit for its employees and their families—exploded into being.

The initial spark for the program had been provided by Norman Miller, chairman of Interstate Batteries. In 1988, Norm was becoming increasingly concerned about the effect of heavy travel on the families of his company's salesmen. They were on the road twenty-one weeks out of the year, usually for about five and a half days at a time.

There was no question that travel was required. Without it, Interstate would be out of business. At the same time, what good would it do to sell batteries if it meant wreaking havoc on couples and breaking up families? That certainly wasn't what Norm wanted Interstate to be known for. Moreover, he knew firsthand the stress of heavy business travel, having spent many years on the road himself.

So Norm asked Jim to see if there wasn't a way to offset the downside of travel. Interstate couldn't take the travel away, but maybe it could at least provide resources to help families cope with the disruption in their home life. In fact, maybe Interstate could help families grow stronger as a result of the travel. Maybe this negative could be made into a positive.

Jim's first impulse was to head to the library to see what he could find on the subject. Nothing. How about the bookstores? Again, nothing!

Then Jim placed a call to Bill Hendricks, a consultant he had recently met. Bill had just finished coauthoring a book on the time demands of businesspeople. Did Bill know of anything addressing

12

the demands of business travel on marriages and families? Bill promised to look into the matter and launched an extensive on-line database search.

Meanwhile, Jim's secretary began calling around to see what she could find. But she and Bill quickly came to the same dead end Jim had. There was almost nothing available on the subject of business travel as it affects the family. This despite a burgeoning mar-

Counting the Cost

The cost of conflicts between work and family life is not borne by employees and their families alone. Employers pay a price as well. According to a 1988 study in *Personnel Journal,* an employer can lose up to 25 percent of an employee's productivity due to personal problems such as marital strife and divorce. If the company loses the employee in the process, that turnover will typically cost the employer an estimated $10,000 to $20,000 or more in turnover costs. An organization with one thousand employees can easily lose as much as $1 million annually due to turnover.

ket for books about marriage and family life! Here and there was a brief article in a business journal or trade publication. But nothing existed that was current or comprehensive.

Key Issues for a Hot Topic

Upon hearing that, Norm told Jim and Bill to develop something from scratch. So we went to work, beginning with a needs analysis. This led to the telling incident at the annual picnic. In the aftermath of that experience, we enlisted the help of the Interstate video department and set up interviews with several groups of Interstate salesmen and their wives. Through these interviews, we identified a dozen key issues.

- Communication when you're apart
- Communication when you're together
- Commitment and trust
- Loneliness, encouragement, and affirmation
- Conflict resolution
- Planning and scheduling
- Finances
- Sexual intimacy and romance
- Parenting
- Saying good-bye
- Re-entry (when the traveler returns home)
- Building a spiritual foundation

Obviously travel affects families in more areas than these. But these were the ones Interstate families wanted addressed. The numerous requests for information and copies of the *Marriage and the Road* materials that we've received from outside the company seem to confirm that these are the critical issues for couples and families everywhere who are affected by business travel.

That's a lot of people. *A lot of people!* According to *American Demographics,* one in five employed Americans takes at least one overnight business trip every year. More than half the country's executives, administrators, and managers travel overnight, as do almost half of its professionals and about 40 percent of its sales staff, technicians, and support personnel.

It's hard to say exactly how many families are affected by these trips. But we do know that neither a person's marital status nor the presence of children in his or her home significantly affects the likelihood that the person will be required to travel. We also know that the typical road warrior is a thirty-nine-year-old male who is married and has a median household income between $30,000 and $40,000. Given that there were 275 million business trips in the United States in 1995—to say nothing of the travel of tens of thousands of military personnel on active duty—it seems safe to say that work-related travel touches the lives of perhaps as many as half of all Americans in at least some way.

It is for these people that we have written this book. What is true for the Interstate sales force and their families is true for countless other road warriors and their families. For many jobs, travel is a necessity. And it won't go away anytime soon, despite the advent of videoconferencing, e-mail, the Internet, "intranets," and other sophisticated means of communicating. (There's evidence to suggest that overall business travel will actually *increase* as a result of these technologies.)

There are plenty of books available on each of the twelve issues listed earlier. But there are almost no resources dealing with these matters from the standpoint of travel, which creates its own unique challenges. So in this book we hope to do something a bit different. While other books go into more detail about the issues of marriage and family life, this book looks at how travel affects those issues, and how travelers and their families can respond in ways that preserve and strengthen their relationships.

Here's How You'll Benefit

This material is born out of years of experience of couples and families, not only at Interstate, but outside the company as well. It is also the product of ongoing research into data about American business travelers, changes in the marketplace that affect them, and how travel is viewed by spouses and loved ones.

So what do we hope to accomplish? What will you gain by reading this book? Here are four practical benefits.

1. You'll become more aware of how travel affects your marriage and family. Believe it or not, not all travelers appreciate the effect their trips have on their loved ones at home. And even those left behind, while often keenly aware that travel is interfering with their lives, can't always put a finger on exactly what's wrong.

This book can help. A problem defined is a problem half-solved, and we'll define some of the problems that travel creates for families. Doing so will especially benefit men, who still do the lion's share of business traveling. Not to be sexist about it, but is there any real disagreement that men by their nature tend to be less

15

aware (some would say clueless) about the finer points of relationships? For some men, this book will come as a wake-up call, warning them that while they are soaring to great heights on the road, their relationships with their wives and children are headed off a cliff.

2. *You'll realize that you are not alone in your struggles to balance the demands of business travel with the needs of your family.* This book is for both the spouse who travels and the one who doesn't. Whichever you are, it's easy to feel that no one understands how the travel is affecting you. Perhaps you look around and see others in similar circumstances, and travel doesn't seem to bother them. So why does it bother you?

In this book, you'll discover that there are *millions* of people who share your struggles. But for a variety of reasons, those struggles are seldom addressed by marriage and family experts, or, for that matter, by industry leaders—at least not realistically or creatively. We're hoping that the information here helps open up dialogue.

3. *You'll find practical advice on how to minimize the effects of travel on your relationships.* This isn't a book of abstractions. You'll meet real people who have dealt with the travel experience—some successfully, others not so successfully. But from the lessons they've learned comes a wealth of practical knowledge that you can use to your advantage. Every chapter contains at least a half-dozen pointers gleaned from the "battle."

Not that we've given rules for how to run your life. These are suggestions that you can adapt to fit your needs and your situation. And every situation is different. What applies to someone else and his or her family may not apply to you. The impact of travel varies widely, depending on factors such as: age of the traveler and of the traveler's spouse and children; extent of the travel; experience with the demands and dynamics of travel; special needs in the family; and the personalities involved.

4. *You'll be challenged to use the time you do have together to work at building a strong, solid marriage and family life.* The best defense is a good offense. Thus the best way to strengthen your marriage and family to withstand the rigors of the road is just that—to *strengthen* your marriage and family. That means build-

ing healthy habits into your relationships, quite apart from travel. We're going to be cheerleaders toward that end.

But what if your marriage is already in trouble? What if your family life is already on the rocks? In that case, your needs may go beyond what this book can provide. You may need to turn to professional counsel to find out exactly what the trouble is in your home, and to find ways you might deal with it.

As you do, keep in mind that travel is rarely the root problem for a marriage or family. Travel merely aggravates whatever problems are already in the home. So if travel is causing you and your loved ones headaches, take a long, hard look at what else is going on. You may discover that those nasty business trips are actually helping to raise some fundamental issues that need to be addressed.

Well, they're calling for our "departure." Are you ready to get started? We're going to begin with one of the key areas of any relationship—communication. Travel *definitely* puts a strain on communication. But in the next chapter, we'll find out how to stay in touch even when you're out of reach.

2

Sorry, but Your Call
Can't Be Completed As Dialed

Communication When You're Apart, Part 1

*D*id you know that the first telephones came with printed instructions on the proper thing to say when using them? The instructions actually gave users a script to follow to get the conversation started. In fact, the convention of saying hello when picking up the phone dates to that era.

That sounds a bit silly now. Today, even children take to the phone as instinctively as birds take to flight. Yet how many traveling spouses could stand a bit of instruction on phoning home when they're out on the road? Here's an illustration of what we mean.

Where's Marsha?

It's Thursday evening, about seven o'clock Pacific standard time. Marsha, a troubleshooter for a software firm, is on the road and she's beat. She has spent all week trying to solve a problem in a client's customized system, with disappointing results.

Not that things started out that way. When she arrived on Monday, Marsha quickly tracked down what she thought was the source of the trouble. She felt she might have it fixed by the end of the day, or Tuesday at the latest. Yet by Tuesday evening, the problem persisted, and two other snags in the software surfaced. On Wednesday, Marsha didn't feel well, so she had trouble concentrating.

Today went somewhat better until her client's information manager started putting pressure on her to get his system up and running by the end of the week. That pushed her to make a frantic call back to headquarters in Boston to get some direction. But to her dismay, she learned that her boss was accepting a position at another company and was off settling details.

All in all, Marsha feels pretty discouraged. She knows that her husband, Tim, is expecting a call tonight. But lying on her hotel bed, Marsha feels too tired to talk to anyone—even her family. "Besides," she thinks to herself, "it's already past ten there. Tim's probably already gone to bed. I mean, he's got to be tired from his job, plus he's got the kids to worry about. I'll call in the morning."

Meanwhile on the East Coast, Tim has been cleaning up the kitchen after putting the kids to bed. So far, his stint playing "Mr. Mom" has gone okay—not great, but not bad. He certainly hadn't bargained on Marsha being gone the whole week. But he's resigned himself to expecting the unexpected when it comes to her job.

Now, as he puts dirty dishes in the dishwasher and wipes down the kitchen counter, he glances at the clock on the microwave. Ten o'clock, and still no call!

"Where is Marsha?" he mutters through clenched teeth.

Tim saunters into the den and flips on the TV, killing time as he waits for her call. But it never comes. Finally, at ten-thirty, Tim heads for bed. As he turns out the light, he wonders where Marsha is, what she's up to, and why she hasn't called. Drifting off to sleep, he makes a mental note to take this up with her as soon she gets home—hopefully tomorrow night.

Trouble's Brewing

When you travel, do you ever decide, as Marsha has done, not to call home? We've heard dozens of veteran travelers admit to this. They know they ought to call. But for a variety of reasons, they don't. Here are three common excuses.

1. *"I'm usually too tired when I get back to my hotel."* It's the same feeling you have when you come home at the end of a long day: You don't want to be bothered; you just want to collapse. Of course, on the road it's a lot easier to avoid contact.

2. *"Phoning home always seems to drag me into a problem."* One husband told us, "There's always a bill that we can't pay right now, and I'm like, why is she even telling me this? I can't do anything about it. A thousand miles away from home, what am I supposed to do?"

3. *"Sometimes I feel too discouraged."* If you've failed to meet your sales quota, if the deal you came two thousand miles to clinch falls through, if the convention speaker you paid to hear canceled at the last minute, you may feel too low to pick up the phone. Even though your spouse and family can be your greatest source of support, it may seem as if it would take too much energy to call.

And that's really what phoning home takes—emotional effort. Remember the old Bell Telephone slogan "Reach out and touch someone"? They had it right. Phoning home means reaching out to touch a loved one. It's a relational, emotional act. For a hard-charging traveler in a task-oriented environment, that may feel like too much to handle. That's certainly the way Marsha feels.

But think what Marsha is communicating to Tim—whether she means to or not—by not placing the call. She's telling him that he doesn't matter. She's leaving him in the dark about where she is and what she's up to, which can only raise questions in his mind as he waits for her call. She's also locking him out of her life at a moment when she could use his support and encouragement.

In short, Marsha's decision not to call, as understandable as it may be, harms her marriage in a small but significant way. If that becomes a pattern for her, watch out!

The Importance of Staying in Touch

Let's find out from some seasoned couples how to maintain communication when travel pulls you and your spouse apart. We might begin by asking, What's the big deal? Why is staying in touch so important? The answer may seem obvious, yet many a traveler manages to overlook it. So let's take a moment to consider what a phone call means when you or your spouse is on the road.

Staying in Touch Maintains Trust and Security

Trust is the bedrock of marriage. Without it, you don't really have a marriage—certainly not a healthy one. But trust not only must be earned, it must be maintained. How else can that happen except through regular communication? Communication is one of the keys to a good marriage. So anything you can do to improve the way you stay in touch during periods of travel will strengthen every area of your relationship.

One wife described staying in touch as "love on the phone." What an apt expression! You see, a call is more than words. The act itself demonstrates that you are paying attention to your mate, that you are breaking away from the demands of work to spend some time with him or her.

Staying in touch is a relational issue, not a chore. If it does become a chore, if calling your spouse is just one more item to check off your to-do list, then you really need to reflect on the quality of your relationship. Something's gone stale, and you may be headed for trouble.

Staying in Touch Helps Overcome Loneliness

It is normal to experience separation as loss. Oftentimes the spouse left at home feels this loss when his or her mate leaves for a trip.

"When Judd first started traveling, I'd drop him off at the airport," one wife said. "Before I even got out of the airport, I had tears streaming down my face. It took me a while to realize that I was grieving, and that whenever he left, I started feeling alone."

That can happen for the traveling spouse, too, especially after he or she has been away for several days. "When I'm on the plane to wherever I'm going, I'm thinking about the trip and my client and what I'm going to do when I get there," says Julia, a lawyer

21

who travels extensively. "I'm all business at that point. But put me in some hotel for a few days with nothing to do all day but legal stuff, and I can't wait to get back home with Jack. If he's not there when I call, it just feels so empty."

Some veteran couples say they've learned to get past the loneliness of travel. Perhaps, but it's more likely that they've just developed ways to cope with it. Phone calls are one of the most important means. They help to remind both partners that the relationship is still intact even though they are separated by hundreds or even thousands of miles. Later, we'll talk more about ways to surmount the feelings of loneliness associated with travel.

Staying in Touch Provides Accountability

By *accountability* we mean a sense of responsibility to your spouse and your marriage. Let's face it: It's easy to become self-centered, preoccupied with your own needs, desires, and agendas. That's especially true when travel puts distance between you and your mate.

But if your marriage is to be a healthy partnership, you need to value your partner and concern yourself with his or her needs, even when he or she is not around. That's the value of a phone

Communication Is the Key

A survey of divorced men and women by Lynn Gigy and Joan B. Kelly found that 79 percent of men and 78 percent of women felt that "growing apart or losing a sense of closeness" was their biggest reason for divorce. The second most common reason, indicated by 60 percent of men and 73 percent of women, was "a feeling of not being loved and appreciated." The bottom line? Married couples need to make communication one of their highest priorities (*Journal of Divorce and Remarriage*, no. 18, 1992, pp. 169–87).

call: It demonstrates that you haven't forgotten what matters. It proves that you are willing to make *time* for the relationship. And as psychologist and marriage expert James Dobson has noted, time reserved for meaningful conversation is crucial to building a relationship.

Whatever else marriage is, it's a contract and a commitment—what some call a covenant. That demands accountability. Suppose we leased you office space and took your money every month, but otherwise you never heard from us. When something broke, you would call, but we would always be out. We never returned your calls. We never inspected the premises. Except for cashing your rent checks, we were phantom landlords. Would you feel we were honoring our side of the lease? Would you want to keep doing business with us? Probably not.

Yet how many travelers—especially men—remain incommunicado for days at a time, then suddenly breeze through town just long enough to change their socks before they're off on another junket! What sort of marriage is that? Where's the accountability?

Staying in Touch Provides a Chance to Deal with Practical Matters

In our scenario, Marsha is the spouse who travels, and Tim has accepted that (for now) as part of her job. But more often than not, it's the wife who is the home-based partner of the team. She is likely holding down a full-time job and inevitably works the infamous "second shift" of keeping the house, raising the children, juggling the finances, and providing a lot of relational glue to the family. That's a lot of responsibility, and it creates a lot of stress.

One thing that could help any wife in that situation would be the opportunity to talk with her husband during the day. If he doesn't call, he frustrates her. He places her in a position in which she has to make all the decisions and take all the responsibility.

"But what else can I do?" the traveling husband might ask. A thousand miles away, with alligators of his own to fend off, what is he supposed to do about situations at home? The point is not that he should try to solve every problem via long-distance phone calls; rather, he should provide support to his spouse as she han-

23

dles them. She needs his input, his preferences, and, most important, his reassurance.

Of course, the same is true if the traveler is the wife (as nearly 40 percent of business travelers are) or if both spouses travel. Marriage takes teamwork, and teamwork takes communication.

How can you maintain that communication when travel forces you apart? In the next chapter, we'll consider some practical strategies for keeping long-distance love alive.

Long-Distance Love

Communication When You're Apart, Part 2

*A*s we've seen, there's a *lot* riding on a traveler's phone calls home. Not that there aren't other means of staying in touch. In fact, we'll look at a few of those in a moment. But for most people, the phone is the number one means of communication.

So how can you make your calls work for your marriage? How can you maintain "love on the phone"? Based on what seasoned travelers and their spouses have told us, we've concluded that effective calls aim at four important objectives. Not every call involves all four. But overall, you want your calls to work together toward the same basic purpose—communication with your mate.

1. Phone Calls Need to Communicate Feelings

Have you ever unintentionally overheard someone's phone conversation with his or her spouse? We have, and sometimes we've been delightfully embarrassed as the caller entered into a rather intimate exchange. (Naturally, we had the good sense to leave and give the person some privacy!)

But we believe that's the exception rather than the rule. It's amazing how cold and businesslike some people can be to their spouses and children. Why, they put more effort into ordering a pizza than they do into catching up with their families!

"When my dad gets on the phone, I can predict what he's going to say," reports one teenager with a sigh. "How's school? How's my basketball team doing? What do I think of our city's football team? And did I remember to put gas in my mom's car? It's always the same. I can count on it."

Not much affection there. A man whose wife travels frequently as an advertising account rep tells a similar tale, though he stops short of outright bitterness: "Sharon and I talk about . . . oh, let's see. She always wants to know how my day went, whether I got done what I wanted to get done. She asks what I had for dinner. She asks about the cat. [Pause.] She asks whether her mother called. [Nervous laughter.] I guess you could say that Sharon and I have a . . . well, a 'functional' relationship. [Laughter.] No, no, we really do love each other."

But is that love *expressed* on the phone? As long as the conversation remains at the level of chitchat, it's little more than what might occur between strangers. We don't recommend that you try to manufacture feelings of tenderness. But you might conduct an "emotional audit" of your recent conversations by asking, What did I reveal about myself and my feelings? What part of myself did I give to my spouse? Or was I all business? Did I just stick to facts and trivialities?

On the other hand, you can't give what you don't have. If you find communication difficult on the phone, it may be because, in fact, communication is difficult when you and your spouse are together at home. It's just that at home, in familiar surroundings, the problem may not be as evident. So if you're having trouble communicating during travel, consider that a litmus test for the level of intimacy between you and your spouse.

2. Phone Calls Need to Communicate Support

If there's one feeling, more than any other, that travelers and their spouses look for from their mates, it's a feeling of support.

"Even when I'm having a good week, I can't wait to call," says Kevin, a salesman, "because the first thing [my wife] asks is, 'How are you doing out there?' I need that kind of support from her, because if I'm having a bad week, I can tell she feels for me. I don't know—when I'm having a bad week, I think of her and the kids more than before. I guess it's human nature, but it's like you're looking for that support."

A similar plea for support comes from a wife telling about her traveling husband. "This past week he gave me his check to disburse. He's like, 'See ya'll next week!' And here I am with the bills, going, 'Okay, which ones can I pay?' And the kids are screaming.

"So then he calls and says, 'Well, honey, how're ya doin'?'

[She glares in exasperation at an imaginary phone receiver.] "'How am I doing?!'"

[Then in her husband's tone of voice:] "'What did you do today?'

"'What did I do today?! I've got two kids and I'm home all day long, and you want to know what I did? Where do you want me to begin?'"

Here's a woman looking for something that her husband can provide like no one else in the world—support. She's not asking him to take away the bills or the mayhem of screaming children. She just wants to know that in the middle of the fray, he understands and cares.

Her situation is instructive because it illustrates so well that work and family are different worlds. On the road, a traveler doesn't hear the children or see the stack of bills. On the other hand, the home-based partner doesn't wake up in a city full of strangers. Their experiences are so different that they might as well be on different planets.

So how can they communicate love on the phone? The traveling partner can start by disengaging from the intensity that usually goes with business travel. A sales rep named Kirby explains, "I have a tendency of coming in at the end of a day, tossing my briefcase down, plopping on the bed, and saying, 'Whew! Well, let me call home.' I grab the phone. Dit, dit, dit, dit. Then it hits me: I'm still sitting there in my work clothes, tired and beat. I'm still tensed up and real defensive.

"What I need to do is to come in at the end of the day, clean up, watch TV, maybe go to dinner, relax a little, and just unwind before I call. I call home too much right when I get in the door. It's almost to the point where I think, 'I need to get this over with.' Instead, I need to say, 'Hey, I'm going to take a few minutes here and clean up, and then call when I'm calmed down.'"

Once he calms down and finally calls home, he can go to the next step by *listening* to his wife—not just letting her carry the conversation while he throws in an occasional "Uh-huh" or "Yeah" but inviting her to unburden herself a little bit. He can ask her not only *what has happened* at home and at her job but *how she feels about it*. That's really what matters—her experience of the situation.

How is it that so many of us can communicate well with clients and sales prospects but not with our own spouses? We come up with all kinds of strategies that invite customers to open up and tell us about themselves. Can't we make a similar effort with our mates? Why not transfer those impressive communication skills into our marriage!

Of course, if you are the spouse at home, who knows what you will be facing at the moment your partner's call arrives? Phone calls by nature are an interruption. You may be working on a particular project or have kids in the bathtub or be thinking about some problem at work, when suddenly the phone rings, demanding your attention and disrupting whatever you're doing. So you also may need to disengage a bit from the immediate circumstances in order to reorient yourself to your mate and your relationship.

One way to ease your spouse into the situation at home is to avoid unloading the truck when he or she calls. Thinking back to the scenario in the last chapter, suppose Marsha calls home and Tim starts off with, "Where have you been? I've been waiting all evening for you to call! I've got kids to feed here, and you didn't get enough groceries!" If she had to face that every time, could anyone blame her for not calling home?

Bill's mother, Jeanne, has become something of an expert in this regard. Bill's father, Howard, travels extensively, and Jeanne has taken Howard's calls under every conceivable circumstance. Her conclusion? "I want him to call again. I don't want that, every time he calls, he's going to be saying, in effect, 'Okay. Here I am. Give me a report. What's wrong now?' I want him to feel that it's a privilege to call home. And even though he may be expecting some bad news, I'm going to find out first how he's doing, and then in a timely way drop in those negatives that are sure to be there from time to time."

There are always practical matters to be discussed, as we're about to see. But what really matters in the relationship? A stack of bills? A flat tire? A bad report card? Surely not! Vastly more important is what goes on inside and between you and your mate— the perceptions, the feelings, the concerns, the desires, the frustrations, the wounds, the pain that you bring to each other. Phone calls from the road may deal with lots of other things, but if they never deal with these, you have cause for concern about how deep your relationship really is.

3. Phone Calls Need to Communicate Information

Ultimately, of course, phone calls do need to address practical, day-to-day situations. That may seem obvious, since most calls probably operate at this level. But the point is that love deals with external realities as well as internal ones.

This especially pertains to planning and scheduling. "I can't wait for tomorrow, Mom," says Anna's daughter, Michelle, as the teen drives her mother home from the airport.

"Tomorrow?" Anna asks, puzzled. "What's tomorrow?"

"You know, my gymnastics tournament. Don't you remember? I told you about it on Tuesday."

Anna suddenly remembers that Michelle did in fact tell her about the tournament, but Anna didn't bother to pull out her appointment book and write it down. Now she's in trouble, because she booked something else for that time.

If only Anna would devote the same energy and concentration to her family that she does to her work! All she has to do is jot down a few reminders. Sure, family and marriage are far more than a checklist of responsibilities. But there is a "business" side to the home that parents and couples cannot afford to ignore.

One woman called home and learned that an overdue notice had arrived from a credit card company. Her husband was rather upset, as he tended to be whenever financial tension mounted. She felt nothing of the sort, since she knew she had mailed in the payment. But to ease her husband's anxiety, she immediately phoned the credit card company. By taking five minutes to do that, she was able to call her husband back and explain the situation. That helped his week go a lot better.

"I can't be bothered with every little detail of what's going on at home," some travelers say. Of course not. But what that means to their spouses is, "I can't be bothered with the day-to-day realities of your world." Can a marriage grow with that attitude?

4. Phone Calls Need to Address Decisions

That last illustration brings us to another aspect of phoning home—decision making and crisis management.

Sometimes it seems like tempting fate to book oneself on a business trip. "It seems like anything that's going to go out goes out when I'm out of town," one husband laments. "The refrigerator, the washer, something's wrong with the car, the kids are sick. It never happens when I'm at home. It always happens when I'm out of town!"

Is that your experience? If so, that's another important reason for keeping in touch. Situations are bound to come up in which you need to make a decision and respond with action.

Yet travel makes it hard to do that. For one thing, distance makes it easy to ignore problems at home. Out of sight, out of mind. But that only pushes responsibility onto the home-based spouse.

There are at least four alternatives to handling crises and decisions on the road.

1. Make a Mutual Decision

Make time for discussing the situation completely, and come to a mutual decision as to what to do. Say, for example, that it's winter and the furnace quits working. You can't wait three or four days to figure something out. You have to act quickly. Let's assume that the husband is the traveler in this instance. When he calls home, he needs to be told exactly what the situation is. Then together he and his wife can talk about what to do.

Both of us have faced that type of situation on occasion, and we wanted nothing more than to just blow it off and let our wives worry about it. But that's life. If we're to be responsive partners, we have to make time to decide with our spouses what we're going to do.

By the way, one prescription for dealing with disasters is to keep a phone book of friends and professionals who can be called when the unforeseen strikes. That can help to remove the demotivation that some travelers have for calling home: fearing what news may await. It can also help the phone call go more smoothly, since problems have already been anticipated to some extent. Most importantly, it reassures the spouse at home of the traveler's love, support, and concern for the home front, even though he or she has to be away.

2. Let the Home-Based Spouse Decide

Trust the home-based partner to handle things on the home front as best he or she can. Let's suppose the traveler doesn't call home, yet the situation calls for immediate attention.

One woman arrived home from shopping, opened her back door, and screamed as two or three inches of water gushed out. Her washing machine had burst a hose. In a panic she dialed 911, and the fire department promptly sent out two trucks and a rescue team.

Later, her husband called her from a distant city. "What did you call the fire department for?" he cried. "Why didn't you just call a plumber?" But you see, that's what *he* would have done had he been there. He wasn't, and it was up to her to deal with the situation. He needed to trust her to respond as she saw fit.

3. Delay a Decision

Sometimes you need to delay a decision until the traveler returns home and things can be discussed at length. Fortunately, not every decision has to be made in a crisis. A woman who was demonstrating cosmetics at a trade show learned that her teenage son had received another failing report card, his third in a row. The parents had tried all kinds of strategies to help the youngster improve, but to no avail. The father was in a rage and wanted to ground the kid on the spot. But the mother wisely told him, "Honey, let's wait until I get home. I want to talk with him, and I want to talk with his teachers again. We've got a problem here, and there's no point in being hasty." Her counsel probably avoided some emotional damage to the youngster, whose difficulties turned out to be physically related.

4. Prepare for the Unforeseen

An Interstate Battery salesman sheepishly admitted to us that one time he called home only to learn that his wife had had to replace the battery in their car. "And I sell batteries!" he moaned. He had known for months that he needed to replace it, but who got stuck with a dead battery? His wife!

Travel has a way of making a person selfish by making it easy to avoid responsibility. While the rest of the world manages to keep up with things like getting the car inspected, filing income taxes, raking leaves, or scheduling household repairs, the traveler finds it easy to push demands like those aside with one of two rationalizations: (1) "I've got to go out of town. I'll do it when I get back"; (2) "I'm just getting back into town. I deserve a break. I'll do it later." Both attitudes only increase the likelihood that problems will crop up at the worst possible time—when he or she is on the road.

Some Tips

Here are a few suggestions for keeping in touch.

Let the Traveling Spouse Primarily Make the Calls

In our experience, it tends to be easier for a traveling spouse to find a way to call home than for a home-based spouse to contact his or her partner on the road. That's because the traveler is usually a "moving target," now in one city, now in another, one moment on a plane, the next in a cab. That puts the burden mostly on the traveling spouse to stay in touch.

Of course, this means that the home-based spouse must exercise a bit of patience, understanding, and flexibility as he or she waits for a call. Travelers usually have minimal control over their circumstances, so placing a call may be a catch-as-catch-can proposition.

Schedule an Approximate Time to Call

Scheduling calls may seem obvious, but countless couples ignore this simple strategy. By doing so, they are letting fate determine the frequency of their communication.

However, one word of warning to the home-based spouse: Don't get bent out of shape if the call doesn't come through, or if it doesn't come through exactly when you expected it. As we've just pointed out, travelers often can't control their circumstances. So the call they promised to make (or to be somewhere to receive) between 5:00 and 5:15 can get torpedoed by who knows what: a meeting that runs late, a traffic jam, even a lost room key.

It's because of things like these that wise travelers and their spouses have learned to spell *sanity* f-l-e-x-i-b-i-l-i-t-y!

Think Ahead to the Next Phone Call

Experienced travelers and their families also learn to develop a "rhythm" to their communication. For example, one woman has learned to expect calls from her husband in the early morning, before he gets involved in the day. Another couple has found that lunchtime tends to be the best time for attempts at phone contact. Still another couple invariably talks in the late evening.

By being aware of the rhythm of your calls, you can think ahead to the next "scheduled" call and anticipate things that might interfere. For instance, a woman on the road who normally calls at the dinner hour might tell her husband, "I probably won't be able to call tomorrow. We'll be driving back from a site visit, and it will probably be late when we get in. Plus there's a two-hour time change. I'll try and call the next morning."

Information like that is so simple, but it can make a big difference in adjusting everyone's expectations.

Minimize Distractions

If a phone call home is your primary means of staying in touch with your spouse, then make the most of that time. Don't let your attention be distracted by a lot of needless "clutter."

For example, if you are sitting in your hotel room, *turn off the TV!* Television distraction seems to be a common problem for men. In fact, some husbands, even when they are home, sit and watch TV while their wives try to communicate with them. They think "listening" and "relating" mean giving an occasional grunt. But that's not communicating—that's insulting! *Pay attention* to your spouse and to what he or she is telling you.

Another common distraction, especially for home-based spouses, is babies and children in the background. If you have a busy family, these interruptions are natural and probably unavoidable. After all, you do have to divide your attention between your spouse and your kids. But it can be difficult to have a meaningful conversation with your spouse when an infant is screaming in your lap or children are tearing the place apart.

Furthermore, it can be downright irritating to constantly be interrupted by your spouse saying, "Wait a second, honey," as he or she pauses to deal with one of the children. After enough of that, you feel like saying, "Look, why don't I call back at a more convenient time?" because it's obvious that not much communication is taking place.

And in fact, sometimes a callback is exactly what is needed. If things are just completely out of control—at either end of the line—there's no harm in hanging up for a few minutes until things have quieted down. One guy had just dialed his wife when the fire alarm went off in his room! Since he couldn't hear himself talk, let alone hear her responses, he wisely shouted that he was hanging up and would call her back. Five minutes later, he did call her back—from a restaurant across the street—and they were able to have an enjoyable conversation.

Call More Often During Times of Need

Calling more frequently when necessary is another tip that may seem obvious. But travelers need to be reminded that not all calls are the same, because not every trip is the same. Some trips come during times that are especially stressful in the life of the family and therefore seem to interfere more.

So as you are preparing for that next business trip, consider the needs in your family. Is there someone who is gravely ill? Is there a crisis at hand? Is your spouse anxiously awaiting news—perhaps bad news? Is there a big event in the life of your kids that you're going to have to miss?

Whenever travel takes you away from an unusually important moment in your family's life, you need to make an extra effort to keep in touch. Your family will probably understand if you can't be there in person to go through the situation with them, but they'll never understand—and may never forgive you—if you aren't there in spirit. A timely phone call home communicates, "I care."

Other Means of Staying in Touch

Phone calls are not the only way to keep up communication. Here are some other means.

Mail

Before the telephone was invented, travelers communicated in writing if they communicated at all. It was a slower medium, to be sure, but in many ways far more powerful. Writing has a way of forcing you to think about what you have to say—and that's a discipline that any traveling spouse could stand to develop.

Still, it's doubtful that many readers of this book will turn to letters and postcards to stay in touch with their spouses and families. They'll have all sorts of reasons for not doing so: lack of time, no stamps, too hard to find a postbox, just not a writer.

But be that as it may, of all the means of communicating from the road, writing has the potential to have the greatest impact on your relationships. Written words come across as though you really mean them. (So make sure that you do!)

Here's a suggestion: The next time you travel, try sending a postcard home, even if you're out for only a couple of days. Trust us—when that card arrives in the mail, it will have an altogether different impact than a phone call. You could describe the place and the people where you are and your reaction to them. Or you could talk about what you look forward to when you return home. Whatever you do, make sure you reveal some part of yourself, some emotion or reaction that is important to you, so your mate has access to *you* as a person.

Put It in Writing

In my travel, it's not unusual for me to be out of the country. These are often long and demanding trips, but they take me to places my family is interested in. One habit I keep is that on the evening I arrive at the foreign hotel, I write a letter home, using the hotel stationery. I mail it that same evening. Normally the letter precedes my return, giving my family information about where I'm staying and how the trip has gone so far. That way, I not only stay in touch with them but allow them to share some of my experience.

Jim Coté

Notes

Some couples leave little notes to each other when travel takes them apart. This works for some, but it's not for everyone. For instance, one wife reported that she and her four children always put cards in the father's luggage, one to open while he's on the plane, one to open the first day away, one for if he's having a bad time, and so on. Meanwhile, he leaves notes around the house for the family to find during the week.

However, another wife tried the same strategy with far different results: "My daughters said, 'We'll make little notes and stick them in the zipper pockets of all of Daddy's suitcases.' Well, when he got home, they asked him, 'Hey, Daddy, did you find our notes?' They wanted him to tell them that he'd found them. But he didn't even open up those parts! It's like he just reached in there to get his socks and underwear. And their hearts were broken. I said, 'We'll never do that again!'"

The lesson is, know your mate!

E-mail

One of the most exciting developments to come along for couples affected by business travel is the Internet. If you work for a corporation, there's a high probability that your company is already on the Net and can furnish you with an electronic mail (e-mail) box. And there are now thousands of service providers who can sign up your family for the "information superhighway." In fact, you may already be "wired" to one of the larger subscriber services, such as America Online.

E-mail has the potential of becoming a valuable tool to communicate with your spouse during a business trip. You can use e-mail to send and receive messages any time of the day or night. That beats the hassles of traditional calling: tied-up phone, broken answering machine, voice mail tag, "Johnny forgot to write it down." It also keeps the spouse on the road from being "unreachable."

Another advantage of e-mail via the Net is that it bypasses long-distance charges (assuming you use a local access provider). The phone companies are fighting that, but for now go ahead and enjoy a chat with your spouse for free, whether calling from Athens, Texas, or Athens, Greece.

Obviously, there are some technical details to worry about—like having the right hardware and software. And there's a learning curve to using the Net. But once you're on and up to speed, you've got a whole new menu of ways to communicate when travel separates you and your spouse.

Sending Flowers and Other Gifts

How can a traveling husband maintain romance in his marriage while on the road? We asked several wives that question, and they immediately said they would love to receive flowers. In the next breath, however, they admitted that although flowers are nice to get once in a while, they are too expensive for their husbands to send regularly.

That's probably true with most gifts from the road. Frankly, a traveler who feels compelled to send a lot of expensive gifts home has to reflect on what the motivation is. Is it for the sake of the home-based spouse or family—or to satisfy some need of the traveler? The number one emotion experienced by frequent flyers is guilt. It would be interesting to know how many flowers guilt has sold. But wouldn't it be cheaper and more effective to pick up the phone and invest a half hour in conversation with your partner?

Company Communications

There are some travelers who are so hard to reach that only their companies can keep up with them. And of course, some military personnel are stationed in classified locales unknown to their families. You have to feel for the spouses and children of people in those occupations, and we're not surprised that the incidence of marital troubles among them is extremely high.

The only thing to say is the obvious: There is no way to effectively relate to your family over time by relying on company-managed communications. Sure, sometimes there's no other way. When the San Francisco earthquake struck in 1989, several Interstate salesmen were working in the area. Because phone service was interrupted, they were unable to contact their families. Eventually, however, word was passed to the company that they were okay, and the company called their anxious families to give them the good news.

But that was unusual. Imagine having your company contact your spouse every time you decided to communicate! How long do you think your marriage would last?

Again, some careers demand that men or women be away from home, unreachable by ordinary means, for extended periods of time. Little can be done to change that. But the individual and his or her family should be forewarned of the severe strain that this isolation is going to put on their relationships, so they can count the costs ahead of time.

There is, however, a practical way that companies can assist business travelers with communication. It would help if, for every trip, an itinerary were furnished to the traveler's family, detailing travel arrangements, schedule, phone numbers, and whom to contact in an emergency. Having this information can help to provide a sense of security to those at home, knowing that they can almost always reach their loved one if necessary.

Good communication on the road has to start with good communication at home. So let's talk about that in the next chapter—unless you happen to be on the road, in which case why not pick up the phone right now and call home?

4

Heart to Heart, Right from the Start

Communication When You're Together

*I*t may seem odd to find a chapter on communication when couples are *together*, given that this is a book about the problems posed by business travel that takes them *apart.* Yet in truth, one of the keys to communicating when one or both spouses are out of town is communicating when they are in town. Here's an example of what we mean.

Monday Night at Tim and Toni's

Tim is an acquisitions editor for a book publisher. He is just home from a grueling ten-day jaunt that took him to six cities. His plane arrived late Sunday evening, and he has spent all day Monday at the office, opening mail, filling out a lengthy expense account, sending out correspondence, and digging through the enormous pile that had accumulated on his desk while he was on the road.

Finally, at about 6:30, Tim calls it a day and heads home, fighting through traffic to arrive at 7:38. As he walks in the door, Toni, his wife, greets him with a brief hug and a peck on the cheek. "Gee,

I was beginning to wonder if I was going to see you tonight," she says with a blend of sympathy and sarcasm.

"So was I," replies Tim. "You know how traffic is on Mondays."

"Yeah. Well, I kept a plate of chicken for you on the stove." She starts preparing Tim's dinner. "Allison had to eat because she was going over to Ellie's to work on their social studies project. And Jeff had a meeting up at school tonight. But I'll sit down with you while you eat."

Tim says nothing. He is engrossed in looking through the day's mail. Finally, as Toni sits at the table, watching Tim's dinner get cold, she asks, "Are you ready to eat?"

"Huh?"

"Are you ready to eat? Your dinner's getting cold."

"Oh, yeah. Sorry. Let me wash up."

Several minutes later, Tim reappears and sits down to supper. After several bites, he mumbles, "Thanks for saving me some food. This tastes great."

"Long day, huh?" Toni asks.

"Yeah. You know how things just pile up while I'm gone. I always get buried!"

"So how was your trip, anyway?"

"Oh, same as always." He pauses. "You said Jeff's at a meeting at school. What is that all about?"

"Well, I think Coach Davis wanted to do some extra work getting the guys ready for the game this week."

"That's right! This week is the big showdown with Watertown High. I'm glad I'm not going to miss this game."

"So am I. Jeff was just heartsick that you had to be away last Friday night."

"So was I."

Suddenly Tim jumps up, grabbing his plate. "Hey, I almost forgot! *Monday Night Football* is coming on." And with that, he moves to the den, where he flips on the TV and tunes in the game just in time for the opening kickoff.

Toni retreats to their bedroom, where she, too, turns on the television. She finds a movie. If the truth were known, she would much rather sit and talk with Tim. She still doesn't know any of the details of his trip. And there are a number of matters she would like to take up with him now that he is back.

"But he's tired," she says to herself. "He needs a night off. I'll talk with him later."

However, it will be the weekend before Tim and Toni find time to sit for half an hour and chat. By that point, many new issues will have come up, and many of the things Toni wanted to discuss on Monday night will have dropped to the bottom of the priority list. Some will have been forgotten altogether.

Sharing Life Together

Who knows how many couples spend Monday nights the way Tim and Toni are spending theirs—together in the same house but miles apart in terms of their communication. Obviously, it doesn't take business travel to keep spouses from connecting with each other. But this scenario is instructive because it shows that communicating at home is more important when one or both partners must travel. Because of travel, there are simply fewer moments to talk and share time with one another. So a couple must make the most of the opportunities they have.

As we've said, communication is one of the keys to your marriage. But why is that? One reason has to do with the nature of communication. To communicate means to share, to hold in common, to participate together. When you sit down and talk with your spouse, revealing some part of yourself, you allow your partner to participate in your life, and vice versa. Communication is a way of *sharing* life together.

And with the stresses and strains of business travel acting to pull your marriage apart, the only way to hold it together is to do just that—to hold it, *together.* Think of your relationship as an enormous tray filled with wonderful, delicious foods served on priceless china and in shimmering crystal. This tray is much too big and far too important for one person to carry alone; it takes two. If either person fails to carry his or her load, the tray is liable to fall to the ground, breaking the fine dinnerware and spoiling a delicious meal. When you and your spouse communicate with each other, you are carrying that tray together.

We Need to Talk

We men especially seem to have a hard time with communication. I'm convinced it's our emotional makeup. We tend to communicate differently than our wives. For example, when I come home from work at the end of the day, I have to fight the temptation to just forget about what has happened rather than relive it by talking about it with my wife. When she asks me to review the events of the day, I often tell her, half kidding, that I'd rather not. Yet I know she needs to know more in order to grow closer to me. I know our communication can strengthen the emotional bond between us.

When I come home from a business trip, I find I easily justify giving her the silent treatment because I've grown used to having my privacy on the road. There, I didn't have to share my feelings with anyone if I didn't want to. I could also have "selective memory"—not like at home, where my wife wants to know it all whether or not I really want to talk about it.

Another unfortunate habit that many of us men fall into is bringing up again and again the troubles of our work, and rarely the joys. But I've discovered that wives are keenly interested in more than just the problems we face. They want to hear about the good along with the bad. They like to hear about the different people we deal with on the job and about our conversations and experiences with them. Oftentimes they are more interested in the relationships we have at work than in the work itself.

Why is that? Again, I believe men and women tend to process life differently. So as men, we're smart to recognize that difference, value it, and respond to it by providing for our wives' needs and not just our own.

Jim Coté

Unfortunately, we have a lot of "breakage" taking place among marriages today because of too many breakdowns in communication. Couples are busy in their work, busy raising kids, busy doing things in the community, busy being with friends—but not busy sharing life together. Add to all this busyness a few days or weeks of business travel, and the relational breakdown can go from bad to worse.

But that doesn't have to happen to your marriage. By striving to maintain close communication with your spouse when you are at home, you'll be able to hold on to a good thing. In fact, you can make a good thing even better, because you'll be building trust and intimacy in your relationship.

It's hard to trust a stranger—but not your soul mate. Not someone with whom you have spent hours in conversation, the two of you allowing each other to unburden yourselves, telling one another about the thoughts and feelings and impressions and questions that swirl around inside. When you enjoy that kind of freedom with your spouse—the freedom to be honest and real—you create a bond that is almost unbreakable, and a trust that is difficult, if not impossible, to violate.

"Hello! Hello! Is Anybody Home?"

However, if you fail to communicate at home, you are almost certain to have ineffective communication during travel. After all, if you're not talking intimately and intentionally with your spouse when he or she is sitting across the table from you, why should things improve when the two of you are many miles apart, linked only by phone?

Marty's relationship with her husband, Ben, suffered for that reason. Marty was a task-oriented doer. As soon as she came home from work, she would busy herself around the house, picking up, cleaning, folding laundry, arranging pillows—whatever she could find to do. Who knows where she found the energy? But she was hopelessly, compulsively active.

As a result, Ben had a hard time getting her to focus on his concerns. "I always thought women were the ones who wanted to talk," he said to a friend, "but not Marty! As soon as I start a conversation, she listens for about thirty seconds, then she sees something that needs to be done, and *poof!*—she's gone."

Ben, a manager for an oil and gas company, used to call home every night when he was on the road. But over time, he began to notice that Marty was giving brief, one-word responses, and that lots of times she would interrupt him with, "Hold on just a second." Then she bought a cordless phone, and he could tell that she was traipsing through the house, "talking" to him while she was working on some task or taking care of the kids. Eventually, Ben got so frustrated with these one-way conversations that he quit calling. Worst of all, he stopped talking when he was at home.

Marty and Ben's marriage never came apart, but it never grew either. Nor did Marty ever seem to wake up to how she was contributing to the lifelessness of their relationship. On a church retreat, she confided to a friend, "Ben is such an independent person, I think I could keel over while he's out of town and I'd be dead for days before he noticed I wasn't answering the phone. He never bothers to call."

Hopefully, you and your spouse will do a better job than Marty and Ben did of talking to each other when you're together, so you'll talk more effectively when you're apart.

Of course, business travel can throw a wet blanket on good communication even before you leave home. Devon came to appreciate that fact. A disaster-claims adjuster for an insurance company, he found that whenever he was gearing up to go out of town, he would usually think of things that he and his wife needed to discuss.

"Some of them were important things," he recalled, "things that really affected, or might affect, our marriage. But then I'd start thinking, 'This is too important to get into just as I'm leaving town. Let it wait until I come back. Then we can sit down and talk about it.'

"But you know, the reality was that when I'd come home, we never talked about it, because even though I'd remember that I was supposed to bring it up, I'd rationalize it the other way. I'd start thinking, 'Hey, I'm just getting back into town. I'm tired. I've got a lot of stuff that's piled up while I was gone. I don't want to get into that just now. I'll wait until things settle down.'

45

"I don't know how many times I went through that cycle before it finally dawned on me that I was letting my travel keep me from dealing with some really big issues in our marriage. When I saw that, I made a decision that every time something important came up, I would set a time with my wife for us to talk about it. Sometimes we'd talk right away; sometimes we'd have to wait until I got back. But getting my wife involved definitely saved my marriage. Even if I got reluctant to bring it up once I hit town, I knew that *she* wouldn't forget!"

Talking the Talk and Walking the Walk

Devon made a wise and practical choice that paid off enormously in his relationship with his wife. How about you? What choices do you need to make to strengthen your communication? If you appreciate the need to stay in touch with your spouse when business travel takes you apart, then the best thing you can do is practice solid communication when you are together at home. Here are some suggestions for doing that.

Make Your Home Conducive to Communication

In recent years, there has been an enormous surge in home offices and telecommuting. However, those who choose that way of operating have discovered that the only way to make it work is to define a work space and establish boundaries to protect their time and privacy. If only couples would be that intentional about creating an environment that fosters communication!

Yet go into some homes, and it quickly becomes clear why no one is talking to each other. No one *can* talk to each other; the home is not set up to allow for good communication.

For instance, here is a couple with young children. Children are a tremendous blessing, but these parents have made the mistake of letting their children dominate everything in the family's life: the conversations, the activities, the schedule, the food, the furniture—everything revolves around the children.

Consequently, whenever Daddy comes home from his travels as a salesman, he can't get five minutes alone with Mommy before one of the kids comes barging in with a question or a problem.

Conversation for this couple comes in sound bites. There are just too many interruptions. As a result, lots of issues never get adequately addressed. Lots of important statements never get said. Lots of understanding never gets to take place. Lots of questions remain unanswered or only partially answered. The kids feel treasured, for sure. But the parents' relationship is severely strained.

What this couple needs to do is periodically fence themselves off from their children and be together *by themselves.* They need to create an oasis for their marriage, a childproof zone in which adult conversation can take place. That will mean learning to say no to some of their kids' demands. But that's okay! The kids won't break. Sure, some parents damage their children by ignoring them. But these parents are hardly in danger of that. If anything, they are damaging their own relationship by letting their kids call the shots.

Another climate that kills open communication is one in which the atmosphere in the home is emotionally stifling. Have you ever been in a home like that? It's a sad place to visit. Every comment is met with criticism. Every question is seized upon as an invitation to a quarrel. Even the simplest of remarks is met with rebuke. And sometimes silence itself is interpreted as an insult.

Just to state the obvious, a home like that is dysfunctional. There is something unhealthy going on. If your household operates that way, we strongly encourage you to seek professional counsel. The issue is not one of assigning blame. The issue is that you and your family are missing out on the good stuff in life—the good stuff inherent in healthy relationships.

Date Your Spouse Regularly

One of the best ways to ensure that you and your partner have an opportunity to talk at more than a superficial level is to schedule a date—once a week if you can, but at least on a regular basis.

Remember how things were before you and your spouse got married? If you were like most couples, you probably couldn't get enough time with one another. You'd go to great lengths to arrange uninterrupted time in each other's company. You went places together. You shared the same activities. You got into long, intense conversations. You talked on the phone by the hour. You were inseparable.

But now?

We're going to say more about the importance of continuing to date one another later, when we discuss sexual intimacy and romance. But for now, let's just say that if communication has broken down in your relationship, the odds are good that a contributing factor is a lack of regular time spent alone together.

So take a trip down Memory Lane to your premarital days. Find someone to watch the kids for a couple of hours. Get out of the house. Get away from the phone (including the car phone). Take a drive. Go to a burger joint. Drive to a park and take a stroll. Be spontaneous. Try something new. Do whatever feels enjoyable and is conducive to conversation. *But do whatever you need to do to talk with your spouse!*

Show Your Love by Attending to Matters While in Town

We mentioned Devon, who had a tendency to put off important conversations because he was getting ready to go out of town—or because he was just getting back into town. The same thing can happen with chores and responsibilities. A traveler can rationalize that because of a trip, his obligations can wait until a more opportune time.

But this is an area in which actions definitely speak louder than words. It does little good to tell your partner how important he or she is to you, only to leave behind a big mess when you travel because you failed to carry out your responsibilities. That creates doubt in the mind of your mate. He or she starts to wonder, "If I'm so important, why was I left holding the bag?"

For instance, we listened as one exasperated wife told us of trying to pay the bills while her husband was off selling merchandise. "Here I've got all these checks to write, and he hasn't deposited his paycheck! I'm like, 'What am I supposed to do?'" You can imagine how that salesman's phone calls home are going to be affected by that little oversight! And just think of the reception he'll get when he walks off the plane!

There's no question that couples do well to adjust their expectations about household chores because of the inconveniences of travel. Maybe the kitchen floor doesn't really need to be mopped

Don't Expect Too Much

One thing that has helped me with my expectations at home is role reversal. Recently my wife and boys went to spend a week at the beach with her sister's family. I had the entire week home by myself to catch up on some business matters. Unfortunately, before my family left, they didn't have time to clean the house. So I found myself grumbling about dirty dishes, dirty clothes, and messy rooms. But by the end of the week, I had the house in tip-top shape.

Then my family came home. Oh, what a joy it was to see them! Yet not thirty minutes after they arrived, I found myself thoroughly provoked as they messed up "my" kitchen, scattered dirty clothes all over "my" floors, and so on. But as I started complaining, it dawned on me how Brenda must feel when I come home from a trip and start messing up "her" house. As a result, I gained a new appreciation for what she has to put up with—and a new realization of the unrealistic expectations I tend to have about the housework. All in all, the experience generated a lot more sympathy, sensitivity, and intimacy because I learned to understand her role a bit more clearly.

Jim Coté

and waxed quite so frequently. Maybe the storm windows can afford to go a few more weeks without a washing. Maybe the car can wait a few more miles before the oil is changed.

But some things really do need to be done. Every couple will have to decide together what those things are and prioritize them. But whatever they turn out to be, *they need to get done!* It's just irresponsible to use travel as an excuse for avoiding the "hassle" of doing them.

Sure, you are snowed under, trying to get things ready for your trip. And sure, you are tired when you're just getting home and would really prefer a rest. But genuine love involves commitment and trust, and by doing your chores, you communicate both. You show your partner that he or she can count on you—not just when you have plenty of time but when you have little time; not just when you feel like doing it but when you would rather be doing something else.

Use Available Company Resources to Keep Your Spouse Informed

One practical aspect of communicating while at home is to keep your spouse in the know about your work. Not that he or she needs to know every detail of what is going on, but you want to keep him or her informed about your schedule and plans, and of course everything that might directly affect him or her.

However, we humans sometimes have a tendency to forget those little details that can prove so important to our mates. For example, a couple will be chatting at dinner, and one of them will say something like, "While I'm in Portland next week, I'm planning to leave the car for servicing."

"Portland?" the other will reply. "You never told me you were going to Portland."

"I didn't?"

"No! I've got a dinner planned for next Thursday night. Remember? I told you about it last month. You said you would put it on your calendar! Now you're saying you'll be in Portland!"

Oops!

None of us will ever totally eliminate slipups like this one, but we may be able to minimize them by using the resources of communication where we work. For example, Jim has arranged for his secretary to print out his calendar each month for his wife, Brenda. She also prepares a memo for Brenda whenever Jim schedules an out-of-town trip. The memo details when Jim will be gone, where he'll be going, what airlines he'll be flying, where he'll be staying, and other particulars that can help Brenda plan.

With the proliferation of communication technologies—fax, voice mail, e-mail, pagers, and so on—there are more ways than ever to keep your spouse updated. These technologies will never be able to substitute for intimate conversation. But they sure can help avoid those nasty surprises that land you in the doghouse.

Monday Night Revisited

In light of these suggestions, let's imagine a different outcome to Tim and Toni's Monday night fiasco. We'll pick up the action with Tim walking through the door at 7:38.

"Gee, I was beginning to wonder if I was going to see you tonight," Toni says. She gives her man a quick hug and a peck on the cheek.

"So was I," replies Tim, pulling her back toward him for a longer embrace. "It's good to finally get home for a change. It seems like I've been gone forever! Ten days on the road, then Monday at the office. And you know how traffic is on Mondays."

"Yeah. Well, I kept a plate of chicken for you on the stove."

"You already ate, huh?"

"Yes. I'm afraid Allison had to eat because she was going over to Ellie's to work on their social studies project. And Jeff had a meeting up at school tonight. But I'll sit down with you while you eat."

"Just the two of us! That sounds good. Almost like going out for our weekly dinner. Let me wash up."

Toni gets the food on the table while Tim goes back to their bedroom. He comes back having changed his clothes and freshened up, looking ready to relax.

"Any mail today?" he asks. He sits down at the table.

"Just bills," replies Toni. "And a notice from What's-his-name— that insurance guy."

"Tom Brandon? What did he want?"

"Oh, something about updating our will."

"Oh yeah, I asked him to send me something on that. You know, with the money and stocks I got from Mom's estate, we really need to go over our will."

"Do we have to do that now? I've got so much going on."

"So do I. But you know, Toni, if we don't take care of it now, we might wish we had later."

"Now there's a morbid thought."

"I know, I know. Let's not talk about it right now. I'm bushed. But let's not just blow it off, either. What say we pick out an evening next week to talk about our options, and then I'll make an appointment with Tom."

"Okay. How about Thursday?"

"Well, I've got to go back out on Friday, so Thursday might be a bit hectic."

"Oh yeah, I see that here on the calendar. Your office called a couple weeks ago to make sure I was aware of it."

"Yeah, but I don't want to wait too long. How about Wednesday?"

"Wednesday it is!"

Tim gnaws on a chicken bone for a few moments and then remarks, "Hey, thanks for saving me some food. This tastes great!"

Toni just smiles. "So how was your trip, anyway?"

"Oh, same as always. Lots of meetings. Lots of chasing prospective authors. Lots of hand-holding and kicking the rear ends of the authors we already have. I hate deadlines—almost as much as our authors hate them!" Then he launches into a lengthy description of one prospective author he has met. He talks about her fiction and how much he enjoys her work.

After a while, Toni looks at the clock. "Wow, it's almost nine o'clock. Jeff should be getting home about now. And I just realized—you probably wanted to watch *Monday Night Football*."

"Yeah, I guess. But you know, I'm enjoying the chance just to talk with you. It's been a while."

"It has been a while!"

"I can always tune in for the second half. Besides, it's only a couple of loser teams playing tonight." Tim pauses and then says, "So tell me about your week."

You and your spouse may interact much differently than Tim and Toni. That's fine—just so long as you interact! Obviously, not every conversation will be deep, nor will every discussion be pleasant. But the key to building good communication is to communicate.

And that has to start at home. It has to start by sitting down, eyeball to eyeball, heart to heart, baring your souls and listening to one another. If you pursue that, you'll find it infinitely easier to have effective conversations even when miles and miles of geography stand between you.

5

Out of Sight but Never out of Mind

Commitment and Trust

*T*here is probably nothing more important to your marriage than commitment and trust. They are the foundation on which your relationship either stands or falls. With them, you can surmount anything. Without them, you don't really have a relationship.

Let's look in on one couple whose commitment to each other is about to be sorely challenged.

The Back Rub

Larry is a salesman who is on the road for days at a time. This trip has been a great one for Larry—maybe the best he's ever had! Just today he wrote a major order for a brand-new client that could double his commission for the month.

So when Larry gets together after work with two other reps from his firm, he is ready to celebrate. One of the guys, Tom, has also been enjoying a pretty good sales streak. But their partner, Hank, feels pretty discouraged.

In an effort to cheer Hank up as well as enjoy his own success, Larry suggests that the three go out for steaks and then see a movie. Tom agrees and adds a suggestion: Since he's single, he'd like to invite Sharon and Lisa, a couple of old friends who happen to live in that town. That's fine with Larry and Hank.

Before long, the group is enjoying thick sirloins and cold drinks at a popular steak house. Larry and Tom talk up their good fortunes, and the women recall old times with Tom. Even Hank seems more hopeful that things will brighten up soon.

After dinner, Tom points out that it would be cheaper to go back to their hotel and watch something on the movie channel. "We can get some munchies from room service," he says, jumping up from the table and heading for the cashier.

Back at the hotel, Hank decides to do some homework on his prospects for the next day, so he heads to his room. Larry and Tom go with the women to Larry's room to watch the movie. It turns out to be a wild and racy thriller with plenty of sex and violence.

Halfway through, Sharon declares that she's too tired to stay any longer and asks Tom to take her home. But Lisa, who doesn't have to work the next day, wants to stay.

"Larry doesn't mind me staying, do you, Larry?" she laughs.

Not wanting to be a spoilsport, Larry smiles weakly and says, "No, I don't mind."

Tom and Sharon leave, and Larry turns his attention back to the movie. He is lying on his stomach on the bed and after a while starts to drift off to sleep. Then suddenly he feels a gentle touch on his back. Startled awake, he realizes that Lisa has moved next to him and is giving him a back rub.

"Does that feel good?" she asks softly.

To his surprise, Larry hears himself saying, "Yeah, it sure does!" But he knows things are headed for trouble. A choice is staring him in the face: whether to resist this woman's advances or give in to the moment.

Meanwhile, back at home, Larry's wife, Suzanne, is falling asleep in front of the TV. She's feeling pretty good after Larry called earlier in the evening to tell her about the success of his trip.

"I hope he's enjoying this," she thinks. "He's been having such a rough time recently. He deserves a break! Maybe I should surprise him with a cake or something when he gets home." She feels proud of her husband and the way he's providing for their family.

It's All about Trust

This true scenario involves sexual temptation, but there is obviously more to commitment and trust than sexual fidelity. Being committed to your spouse means devotion to him or her in every respect. It means that you have made up your mind to be loyal to the person you have married. Your spouse can count on you to be there and, hopefully, to act in his or her best interests.

These high ideals may sound unrealistic in an age when divorce claims up to half of all marriages and when countless spouses admit to having affairs. But marital commitment is not unrealistic. It may be difficult sometimes. But the fact that you hang in there and work through problems is a sign you can be trusted.

Is that realistic? *Can* you be trusted?

If not, that only confirms what was said earlier: Without commitment and trust, you don't really have a marriage. That's because marriage involves the union of two people, with all their hopes and aspirations, along with their faults and insecurities. When it comes to marriage, a person is basically asking, Is there anybody who will take me as I am—warts and all—and be true to me? Is there anyone I can trust with the deepest, most intimate parts of myself?

Marriage exposes us for who we are. And that kind of vulnerability means we need someone who won't violate our trust by telling jokes on us, putting us down, ignoring us, taking advantage of us, or running off with someone else. If we don't feel confident and secure in the other person's love, we won't be open and honest, and our marriage will lose its intimacy.

High-Fidelity Commitment

Ask those who counsel couples struggling in their marriages, or who have the unenviable task of trying to patch up wounded marriages, and you'll get blunt advice. For example, Kent Hughes says straightforwardly, "Men, our wives must be able to rest in the fact of our fidelity. Everything about us—our eyes . . . our language . . . our schedules . . . our passion—must say to her, 'I am, and will always be, faithful to you'" (*Disciplines of a Godly Man*, p. 43).

Travel—a Test of Commitment

Commitment is one of two themes that come up again and again as we think about the effect of business travel on marriage (the other is communication). Travel *tests* commitment. For one thing, it raises to the surface whatever problems and weaknesses already exist in a relationship.

For instance, say you and your spouse have a hard time holding to a budget. Travel makes it easy to ignore your finances, so you overspend in certain areas. Then, faced with a stack of bills, the two of you get into a terrible fight. You would probably quarrel about money anyway, but travel makes the problem that much worse.

Another way travel tests commitment is that it isolates you from your partner. There's a sense of freedom and independence in jumping in the car or hopping on a plane and heading out of town. Once you pass the city limits, once your plane leaves the ground, your mate is not there to look over your shoulder. He or she has no way to make you responsible or hold you accountable. As far as your marriage commitments are concerned, you are on your own.

That brings to mind the old saying that character is what you do when no one else is looking. Travel gives you a chance to prove your character. You demonstrate what sort of person you are when you don't have to "perform" for your spouse.

Annie learned about this in a most interesting way. She and her husband, Jack, were attending a banquet hosted by his company. During a lull in the program, Annie and Christene, one of the other women at their table, excused themselves to go to the ladies' room.

As they were fixing their makeup in the parlor, Christene turned to Annie and said, "You are such a fortunate woman."

"What do you mean?" asked Annie.

"Well, I mean, to be married to Jack."

"Oh, yes . . . Jack's a wonderful man," Annie replied, uncertain of Christene's drift.

"Oh, he's more than wonderful," Christene went on. "He's a treasure!"

"How do you mean?" Annie asked, taken aback.

Christene smiled and said, "Annie, do you remember when Jack and the rest of us went to that association meeting last month?"

Christene was one of Jack's coworkers, and they frequently collaborated on projects. "We were in meetings all day long, and by the time dinner rolled around, we all wanted to just go out and party. So we went to this restaurant and had a big meal. Then somebody had the idea to go to a casino. Everybody jumped up and said, 'Great idea! Let's go!'

"But while we were waiting for the valet to bring our car, Jack announced that he was going back to the hotel. Everybody was like, 'Aw, c'mon, Jack! We won't stay out too late. Come with us.' But he was real firm. 'I'll get a cab,' he kept saying.

"And then Frank asked him if he was feeling bad, or what. How come he didn't want to come? And I'll never forget—Jack said, 'I want to go back and call Annie. I haven't talked to her all day, and I want to hear about her day.' So he went back to the hotel.

"And I thought, 'Wow! Imagine that! He cares enough about his wife that he would take a cab back to his hotel just to make time to call her.'"

Annie smiled knowingly. That was Jack, all right.

Then Christene stunned her by adding, "I'd give anything if Martin paid attention to me like that. But he only does it if I'm around and make him talk to me."

Again, character is what you do when the choice is completely up to you.

A Chance to Prove Your Love

Travel also tests character and commitment by occasionally presenting temptations. We saw an illustration of that earlier with Larry. Obviously, Larry doesn't have to go out of town to face sexual temptation. But when one is far from home, it seems the temptations are much stronger.

And in a way, that's as it should be. There's a sense in which you don't know how trustworthy you are until you are sorely tempted to violate that trust. A man can talk all he wants about reserving his love exclusively for his wife, but the real test is when an attractive woman makes a pass at him. Then we'll see what his love is made of.

Only time and temptation will prove genuine trust. Business travel presents plenty of opportunities to abandon your commitments—if that's what you want to do. But another way of looking at it is that travel poses plenty of opportunities to honor your commitments—if that's what you *choose* to do.

There is one final way that travel can test a couple's commitment. This one is subtle but important. Because business travel usually is not a shared experience, it introduces distance into the relationship—literally, of course, but also symbolically and emotionally.

Marriage is all about sharing life together, so anything that takes a couple apart works against that. There's nothing wrong with having separate experiences. No couple can share *everything*. But when travel becomes a wedge between a husband and wife, that's a problem.

Marriage experts Gary Smalley and John Trent remind us that "to treasure something means to attach great importance or high value to it. People take good care of what they treasure. . . . People take time with what they treasure" (*Home Remedies*, p. 19). Wise business travelers maximize the time they have at home with their spouses by seeking out opportunities for shared experiences. They also seek creative ways to share their independent experiences with their partners, in order to enhance the sense of interrelatedness.

We're aware that sharing time together is a special problem for businesspeople who travel heavily, for spouses who don't see each other for weeks and months at a time, and for those whose lives are constantly interrupted by trips. It's hard to build a relationship with someone you never see. That's why effort, discipline, planning, and creativity must be cultivated. Travelers and their spouses must *overcome* the liabilities that travel imposes.

Jill was married to an oil executive who was constantly jumping on a plane. One minute he would be in his office. Then the phone would ring with news of a hot prospect across the state. In an instant, he would drop everything and dash to the airport.

Sometimes Jill wouldn't find out that her husband was gone until he called her at midnight to tell her where he was. Supposedly, she got "used to it"—until one day she woke up and realized that she really didn't have a marriage. She had a husband, but so what? She didn't have a *relationship* with that husband. She was just the mistress he visited on the weekends. His real commitment was to the challenges of the road—and Jill deeply resented that.

Churchill's Treasure

Winston Churchill, the gutsy prime minister of England during World War II, was known for his toughness and irascibility. Nevertheless, he had a soft place in his heart for his wife.

Churchill once attended a formal banquet in London, where the dignitaries were asked the question, "If you could not be who you are, who would you like to be?" Naturally, everyone was curious as to what Churchill, who was seated next to his beloved Clemmie, would say. After all, Churchill could not be expected to say Julius Caesar or Napoleon. When it finally came Churchill's turn, the old man, the last respondent to the question, rose and gave his answer. "If I could not be who I am, I would most like to be"—and here he paused to take his wife's hand—"Lady Churchill's second husband" (Kent Hughes, *Disciplines of a Godly Man*, pp. 43–44).

Suggestions for Honoring Your Commitment

In all likelihood, you were asked something like the following question at your wedding ceremony: Do you, (your name), take (your spouse's name) to be your lawfully wedded husband or wife? Do you promise to love him or her, comfort him or her, honor and keep him or her, in sickness and in health; and forsaking all others, to be faithful to him or her as long as you both shall live?

Unless you left your betrothed at the altar, you accepted this vow by responding, "I do." This was your solemn pledge to your spouse, made in front of his or her family, the assembled witnesses, the state in which you were married, society in general, and God.

It can be sobering to reread this vow after having been married for a while. We realize how little we understood of what we were signing up for! And if our marriage is now struggling, we may be tempted to think, "Well, of course I *said* that. But those were just words. The wedding was just a formality. How was I to know that marriage would be so tough . . . that my spouse would turn out to be such a jerk . . . that I would meet someone else . . . ?"

However, wedding vows are *not* just words, and the ceremony is *not* just a formality. Sure, there are those who treat them that way. But even those who go through the motions do so because in fact marriage means something deeply important. Above all, it means devotion to another person. It means formally committing yourself in the ways the wedding vows describe.

Obviously, married people sometimes break their vows, and sometimes the breach is serious enough that the relationship ends in divorce. But let's agree on one thing: At heart, marriage involves a sacred trust. It's a trust that, frankly, none of us is really adequate to uphold perfectly. Yet by honoring it as an ideal, we stand a much better chance of honoring it in practice.

This is the place to begin if we want to honor our marriage vows. We have to *start* with the conviction that those vows are worth upholding, that our marriage is worth fighting for. Because in truth that's what it's going to take—a real fight—to honor our commitment.

Here are some tips for waging that battle.

Identify Your Marriage's Vulnerable Spots

Identify ahead of time the places in your marriage that are especially vulnerable to the stress of travel. Here's a little inventory of

Our Word Is Our Bond

G. K. Chesterton wrote that he "knew many happy marriages, but never a compatible one. . . . For a man and woman, as such, are incompatible." But the purpose of the law, he said, was to hold them together through moments of strain, to give them a second wind. "All human vows, laws, and contracts are so many ways of surviving with success this breaking point" (Hadley Arkes, "Finding Fault with No-Fault," *Wall Street Journal*, April 16, 1997, p. A12).

What's Your Termination Policy?

Maggie Gallagher, in her book *The Abolition of Marriage,* writes, "It is surely an irony of history that at the same time that the law has increasingly rejected the age-old notion that employees are terminable at will, it has embraced the idea that marriages can be terminated at the will of one party. . . . [I]t is legally easier and less risky to dump a wife than fire an employee" (Hadley Arkes, "Finding Fault with No-Fault," *Wall Street Journal,* April 16, 1997).

a few areas in which married couples tend to experience trouble. Put a check next to the items that you and your spouse frequently struggle with.

Communication   Money
Planning and scheduling   Health
Resolving conflicts   Parenting
Sexual intimacy   Family and in-laws
Housekeeping and chores

The areas you have checked are the ones most likely to be affected by travel. Can you think how?

By the way, you might want to compare your responses with your spouse's. If they are radically different, you should both check the first item on the list—communication! It's obvious you are seeing the marriage much differently.

Address Problems in Your Marriage

If you know where the problems and weaknesses are in your relationship, you need to consider: What can I do as a husband or wife, and what can we do as a couple, to strengthen our marriage in these areas?

Don't let travel become an excuse to ignore festering problems. Use it as a reason to address and overcome them. Don't say, "Oh, I can't deal with that now. I'm going out of town" or "I'll worry about that when my spouse gets back." Travel does not delay or diminish trouble—it just deepens it.

Resolve to Be Faithful

Make up your mind ahead of time that you are committed to being faithful to your spouse. Doing so won't make you invincible, but it will put you in the frame of mind to resist the urge to compromise.

Also, it's crucial to recognize your vulnerability. The person who realizes that, given certain circumstances, he or she could be prone to commit adultery is a person who is on guard. But the person who thinks, "Who, *me* have an affair? Never!"—that's the one who is already headed for a fall.

Indeed, one of the most common things you hear from people who have had affairs—especially men—is, "I never thought it could happen to me." Well, wake up! It can happen to you. It can happen to *anyone.*

Once you acknowledge that you can be tempted, it follows that the best way to stay out of trouble is to avoid situations in which temptation is likely to occur. We're not advocating monkish isolation in your hotel room. Just know yourself and what circumstances are safe for you.

Sexual temptation thrives on loneliness and boredom, so take steps to avoid these (chapter 6 offers suggestions). That can be hard to do in a hotel room at the end of a long day, when your brain is fried. But consider doing the things you would do if you were home: Read a book, pursue a hobby, hit a bucket of golf balls, take in a concert, have dinner with a friend—whatever helps you unwind in a healthy way.

What if you are the spouse at home? Be aware that you can be just as vulnerable as your partner many miles away. Audrey felt that her cool, stable temperament precluded her from ever lapsing into an affair. Moreover, she assumed that her career kept her too active and too fulfilled to need anything that her marriage couldn't offer.

But what Audrey failed to consider was how important her relationships at work would become as her husband's work took him out of town more and more. Because he was away so much and the couple did not have children, she found it easier to stay late at the office many evenings. This scored a lot of points with her coworkers, especially the men, who viewed her long hours as a sign of real commitment and toughness. Before long, they were inviting her to join them for dinner, and she eased into a pattern of "closing up the shop with the guys," as she put it.

Had Audrey been asked about the wisdom of these late-night sessions, she would have dismissed any concern. She would have insisted that the purpose was to catch up on important work. But as it turned out, Audrey was in denial about the real reason she stayed so late: She didn't like going home to an empty house and an empty bed.

It took a close call to wake Audrey up to reality. One night, one of the men, Paul, asked if she could give him a ride home, since his car was in the shop. Audrey was glad to help. She and Paul were good friends.

On the way, they got into a deep discussion about some organizational issues in the company and their effect on a current project. When they pulled up to Paul's house, he invited her to come in and finish their conversation over a cup of coffee. She agreed, and for the next hour they talked about the issues at work.

Now the hour was late, and Audrey mentioned that she had to go.

"I know you do," Paul said. "But before you leave, may I ask for some advice?"

"Sure, Paul. What is it?"

Paul then proceeded to tell Audrey a long and involved tale about his former wife. He described their early love, their troubled marriage, her failures as a companion, his attempts to make the relationship work, and the couple's eventual parting. Paul was a gifted storyteller, and Audrey sat transfixed by his narrative. She felt her heart stirring with a wide range of feelings—not least of which were tenderness and compassion toward Paul.

Looking back, Audrey realizes that she should have recognized the danger. But those emotions were so powerful! She had not had those feelings for a man in a long time—in fact, not since she had felt that way toward her husband a number of years before.

Eventually, Paul's memories brought him to tears, and the tears led to a hug, and the hug led to a kiss. And the kiss led to shock, and then to delight, and then to another kiss, and soon Paul was fumbling with the zipper of Audrey's dress. And that's when she woke up.

"No!" she suddenly cried, pushing Paul away. "I can't!"

"Oh, Audrey—" Paul began.

"I'm sorry," she said, standing up. "I shouldn't have stayed. I need to get on home." And she left.

Audrey was mature enough to spend the next few days reflecting on why she had ended up in that situation. And she concluded that she and her husband had been taking their marriage for granted, and it had grown stale. Without realizing it, she had begun to look outside the relationship for that which could only be had inside it. So when her husband returned home that weekend, she made sure they had a long, heart-to-heart talk about the value of their marriage and what was required to sustain it.

One thing they agreed on was a simple but crucial strategy that every couple ought to employ: Stay connected with your spouse. Some travelers do that by carrying a small, framed picture of their mate to put on their dresser or nightstand. And calling home is an obvious way to stay in touch as we saw in chapter 3.

None of these suggestions is guaranteed to shut down sexual temptation. But taken together, strategies like these can be a strong defense against infidelity when you're on the road.

Maintain Communication with Your Spouse

Commitment must be demonstrated, but it also must be *expressed*—which is a matter of communication. When a traveling spouse calls home, it reassures his or her partner that the traveler has not forgotten the relationship. The call itself implies, "You matter to me."

But whether you are speaking from the road or face-to-face at home, make sure you and your mate are not letting business travel squeeze you into separate lives. Invite each other into your experience. Talk about what you are dealing with, the people you are meeting, and especially the feelings you are having. *Listen* to each other, and do whatever you can to pursue intimacy rather than isolation.

In light of all these suggestions, how might Larry deal with the situation described earlier? Let's pick up where we left off.

Larry's Decision

"Does that feel good?" Lisa asks softly.

To his surprise, Larry hears himself saying, "Yeah, it sure does!" But he knows things are headed for trouble. A choice is staring him in the face: whether to resist this woman's advances or give in to the moment.

Larry looks down, and his eyes fall on his wedding band. He thinks of Suzanne and her warm smile and realizes that she is probably fast asleep by now.

He can still hear her last words as he headed out the door for the airport: "So long, honey! Be careful. And don't forget: I'm here for you always!" They are the words she always uses when she sends him off: "I'm here for you always!" Just hearing her voice echo in his ears helps him strengthen his resolve not to disappoint her.

"It does feel good, Lisa," Larry says, sitting up and turning to face her, "but I'd rather not go any further. I don't think my wife, Suzanne, would want me to either."

Lisa's expression shows a mixture of surprise and embarrassment. But she quickly recovers. "I'm sorry. I didn't mean to intrude. You just looked so worn out, and, well, I thought I'd—"

"It's okay," Larry says, cutting her off. "You're right. I am pretty tired. It's been a long day. In fact, it's been a long week. Listen, let me walk you down to the lobby and get you a cab. It's been a great evening, but I need to call it a night."

And with that, Larry opens the door.

A little while later, he returns to his room and gets ready for bed. Before he turns out the light, he opens his wallet and pulls out a photo of Suzanne. "Good night, baby," he mumbles as he stares at her face. "Thanks for being there for me. I'm coming back real soon. Real soon."

Beating the Blues and the Blahs

Loneliness, Encouragement, and Affirmation

*I*f you frequently travel on business, somewhere along the way you have probably heard the comment, "It must be exciting to travel and visit all those exotic places!" Such is the perception of many who are unfamiliar with life on the road. To them, a business trip seems glamorous—practically a paid vacation! But you know better.

Without question, visiting new places can be interesting and even exciting, especially if you're cut out for the job. And for many travelers, there are certain perks that come with the assignment, making it tolerable, possibly even enjoyable.

Nonetheless, there's no getting around the fact that business travel is usually anything but glamorous. It has its own set of rigors that can exact an enormous toll on the traveler—not least of which may be the emotional toll of loneliness.

Some travelers don't like to acknowledge loneliness. In the first place, business travelers as a group tend to be less susceptible to the anxiety that most others would feel in unfamiliar surroundings. Furthermore, for us, as travelers, to admit that we feel lonely on the road can itself cause anxiety. It's the feeling that we're going soft; it's almost an admission of failure, as if we're not up to the challenge of operating solo. What's happening to me? we wonder. I must be slipping!

But in this chapter, let's let our hair down and talk openly, shall we? Nobody likes feeling lonely, but the fact is that travelers often do feel lonely. We may be highly independent and thoroughly resourceful, yet we still find that ache in the chest that signifies loneliness.

And even if by some miracle we're one hundred percent immune to those feelings, the issue doesn't necessarily go away, because our spouse at home may experience tremendous loneliness whenever we have to be away.

Let's explore these matters by considering the case of Cassandra and Michael.

Home Alone . . . Again!

Cassandra pulls away from the toll booth at the south exit from DFW Airport. Quickly rolling up her window to keep out the humid heat of a Texas June, she catches a whiff of jet exhaust that makes her feel mildly nauseous. The car's air conditioner is managing to put out only a lukewarm breeze, and Cassandra silently swears in frustration.

A couple of miles down the road, she realizes she is speeding. She is still racing with adrenaline, having dashed to the airport in time for Michael's 5:14 Sunday afternoon departure. As usual, they arrived just in time, with Michael barely managing a hug and a quick kiss before grabbing his bag from the trunk and sprinting inside. Cassandra is still feeling the tension of it all.

But now she slows down and tries to relax. Why rush home? Nothing much to look forward to there! Dinner in front of the TV. Tomorrow morning, up at 6:00 A.M. and off to work. Come home. Dinner in front of the TV. Same thing Tuesday. Same for Wednesday. On Thursday, maybe she will go out to dinner with a friend or to a movie or to a mall. Then on Friday, Michael will finally be back, and things won't be so . . . lonely.

"I Hate Travel!"

Across the country, long after Cassandra has finished watching TV and nodded off to sleep, Michael is just arriving at his hotel room. He is not a happy camper! Thunderstorms delayed his plane nearly two hours. With the time required for baggage claim and ground transportation, plus the loss of an hour crossing time zones, it is now past midnight local time.

"That's just great!" Michael fumes to himself as he sets his alarm before turning in. "Practically twelve-thirty in the morning, and I have a six-thirty breakfast meeting to get to! I hate travel!"

Michael turns off the light, but he won't get much sleep this night. For one thing, even at this hour other guests in the hotel keep opening and closing their doors, irritating Michael to no end. But the real problem is that Michael is still "wired" from his trip. The dash to the airport, the hurry-up-and-wait feeling of sitting in the terminal during the flight delay, the long flight, the tension of finding transportation to his hotel, the awareness that he must be ready for peak performance come morning—these and countless other factors have saturated his system with adrenaline, so he now finds himself utterly exhausted yet hopelessly wide awake.

Michael has never been to this city before. No one met him when he arrived at the airport. Indeed, he has never met the people he has come to visit. All he has are a couple of names and a phone number. He had glanced at a map of the city in the airport, but since the landmarks were unfamiliar, the layout meant little to him.

As he lies there in the darkness, Michael's thoughts race through the week ahead. It will be a week of constantly meeting new people, constantly having to win their confidence, constantly having to be at his best. Lots of unknowns. No guarantees. No one to fall back on. No familiar faces.

Then Cassandra comes to mind, and he wonders how she is doing. He automatically thinks about what time it is in Dallas. "Eleven forty-five. Way too late to call." But he wishes he could. Just to hear her voice would be reassuring, something familiar and soothing in a strange place.

68

The Hidden Value of Loneliness

Most of us tend to view loneliness as a bad thing. Certainly, it feels unpleasant, as Michael and Cassandra can attest. But have you ever considered that loneliness may actually be a healthy thing? It's a poignant sign that you are human and need other people. Thus, it's natural for you to experience loneliness when travel pulls you apart from your family. Those feelings are a reminder of a profound truth: People are meant to be in relationships. Indeed, the better things are at home, the harder it is to be away or to have someone away.

As human beings, we have a fundamental need for intimacy, a need to *belong*. Emotionally speaking, being close to a community, a group, a family, and ultimately a spouse affords us a place in the world, a spot of identity and security. By forcing us to separate from those we know and love, business travel can prove highly disruptive to that sense of home. We experience a feeling of being lost.

Of course, sometimes we *need* to get "lost" for a while. We need a break from others, even those closest to us. There is truth to the adage that absence makes the heart grow fonder. And even when it doesn't, it at least provides relief from the routine. Indeed, there are probably a few fractious marriages that survive only because frequent business travel keeps the partners apart enough to avoid a meltdown.

The point is, travel tests our relational intimacy in many ways. Oddly, loneliness is the indication that we test positive for wanting to stay connected. So as much as we may dislike feeling lonely, we can at least acknowledge that the feeling springs from legitimate roots: the desire to know and be known, to love and be loved.

"I Need That Support!"

However, just because we may feel lonely doesn't mean we have to stay lonely or be crippled by that feeling. We can fight to maintain our equilibrium. And spouses can help each other immeasurably in this regard by offering encouragement and affirmation—two of the best life preservers when loneliness threatens to drown us.

In fact, when we interviewed the salesmen at Interstate Battery, they all agreed wholeheartedly that without their wives cheer-leading for them, they wouldn't do their jobs nearly as well. One of them said matter-of-factly, "If I didn't have the support from her and the family, it wouldn't be worth it."

Another put it this way: "My wife is always telling me, 'That's great!' Whatever [my quota for the day] is. 'That's great! You'll get 'em tomorrow. No problem!' No matter what I say, it's always, 'Great!' Maybe that's why I call her every night, because I know she's going to say, 'That's great! You're doing a great job!'"

When a traveling spouse feels that kind of support from his or her mate, it's hard to stay lonely or discouraged. Affirmation like that is a real shot in the arm that gives the traveler renewed strength.

Yet all too often, married partners get so wrapped up in their own issues that they fail to communicate encouragement to their mates. For instance, Aaron is so wrapped around the axle playing "Mr. Mom" to his two small children that he doesn't hear the anxiety in the voice of his wife, Maria, when she calls from a distant city.

Maria is struggling to negotiate a deal for her employer—a bargain that has a direct impact on her company's future and, hence, on her employment, which in turn affects her family. She's feeling quite nervous about the impasse reached at the end of the day's discussion. What she really longs to hear is a word of encouragement from Aaron. Instead, he spends most of the conversation complaining about fussy kids, the endless picking up to be done, and a broken washing machine.

Or take Wendy, who has just landed a new account for her advertising agency. Her husband, Lawrence, is also traveling on business, attending a training seminar. As soon as Wendy reaches him that evening at his hotel, she starts crowing over her good fortune. Indeed, she goes on and on in her enthusiasm until finally she concludes, "Well, honey, I gotta run. I'm late for a dinner meeting. But I wanted you to know the good news. By the way, how's your seminar?"

"Okay, I guess," he sighs. "Nothing to write home about."

"Well, you can tell me all about it when we get home. See ya!" And with that, Wendy hangs up. She never gives Lawrence a chance to tell her how he really feels: disappointed that the training sessions are covering material he already knows, angry that he has to be away from home, and terribly frustrated because he is stuck at the training center, which is far from any amenities. His trip is not nearly so bright as Wendy's, and her glowing phone call has not lifted his spirits in the least.

There's nothing wrong with celebrating our triumphs or stewing over our troubles. We always have a right to our feelings, whatever they happen to be. But in the midst of expressing our emotions, it's important to remain sensitive to the needs of our partner. At the very moment we are focused on our own situation, our spouse may need a word of encouragement to help him or her get through a lonely, discouraging time.

Beating the Blues and the Blahs

All kinds of things can stir up lonely feelings for the traveler as well as for the spouse back home (or in some cases, on the road, too). One man told us that just seeing a family at the airport meeting their daddy could raise a lump in his throat and cause him to long for home. Likewise, a woman whose husband is frequently away feels a sense of loss every time she pulls her car into the garage and sees an empty space where he usually parks his car.

What strategies can we use to head off outbreaks of loneliness like these and keep them from spiraling down into serious bouts of grief and even depression? Here are a few suggestions.

Call on Others for Emotional Support

As we noted earlier, loneliness is a symptom of your need for other people. Your spouse cannot be with you on a trip, but are there others to whom you can turn, if for no other reason than relaxing conversation and the pleasure of their company? Obviously, they cannot (and should not) take the place of your mate, nor should they compete with his or her affections. But they can help you get through your journey without succumbing to fits of loneliness.

71

Almost any other human being can serve in this capacity; the main thing is to seek out some company. So Lawrence, the person who was feeling depressed about being at the training seminar, could ask some of the other attendees or one of the instructors to join him for dinner. Likewise, a salesperson visiting accounts in a distant city might invite one of his better clients and his or her spouse out to dinner (although some companies have policies prohibiting this practice).

If you travel a great deal in your work, there is a high probability that you have acquaintances in or near the areas you visit. For one thing, you have probably established relationships in those areas during previous trips. And even if you are visiting a locale for the first time, some of your friends from times past, such as roommates from college or former coworkers, may live in that region. Why not make it a point to call some of these folks (maybe even before you hit town) to see if they are available? Sure, it's going to take some energy and logistical planning to set things up. But the outcome will be well worth the trouble. Seeing a friendly face beats sitting in an empty hotel room watching TV any day! (For most of us, anyway. There are some for whom solitude is an antidote to loneliness.)

These same principles hold for spouses at home as well. Allow family, friends, and others to meet some of your relational needs. That's what seasoned partners of veteran road warriors learn to do. They develop a valuable network of people they can turn to for help and encouragement while their husband or wife is away. They've discovered that other people tend to be quite understanding and supportive. Other people may not appreciate all that is involved with being married to a business traveler, but they instinctively empathize with the feeling of loneliness and are usually only too willing to help out.

"But we just moved into the area," someone may be saying, "and I don't know anyone." Well then, you have an excellent opportunity to start making some friends while your spouse is out of town! So bake some cookies and take them to one of your new neighbors. Or if you have kids in school, call up some of the parents of their classmates, introduce yourself, and arrange to get together. Or find a church or synagogue and start attending, letting people know you are new to the community. You're going to have to initiate the contact. But once others realize you want to be involved, they will probably throw out the welcome mat.

Stay Connected with Each Other

As we have said, no one can or should be expected to take the place of your spouse. No matter how much help and support others are able to offer, it's vital that you and your mate stay in touch. That will take some planning, in light of the many uncertainties created by travel. But you've got to do it! Your partner needs the reassurance that comes from hearing your voice (for more on this issue, review chapter 2).

Of course, there are other ways to stay connected than long-distance phone calls. Many travelers find it helpful to keep a photo of their family handy as a reminder of home. Others make a point to "include" their family in their trip by picking up items that will be of interest when the traveler returns or by visiting some site that holds special importance to their family and reporting on it later.

Getting together with friends whom both you and your spouse have known over the years can be a delightful way of bringing your partner into the emotional experience of the trip. Naturally, your friends will want to hear about how your spouse is doing, and you'll have lots of news from them to share when you get back.

Perhaps some will argue that trying to stay connected with your spouse only increases the possibilities for loneliness. "If I keep thinking about my loved one who is away, I'll start thinking about how he or she is not here, and then I'll start feeling lonely. Better to keep my mind occupied elsewhere." There is some legitimacy in that. As we've pointed out, not everyone experiences or deals with loneliness in the same way. For some, doing things like carrying pictures of the family or listening to tapes of their children's voices is not a good strategy.

You'll have to consider what's best for you. But we're not sure an out-of-sight, out-of-mind approach is a healthy antidote to loneliness. It may be unpleasant to miss your honey, but is forgetting him or her really the best way to deal with that?

We think a much better strategy is to stay in contact as much as possible, realizing that you are a team and must work together to surmount the stress business travel imposes on your relationship.

Be Your Partner's Cheerleader

We can't say enough about how important encouragement and affirmation are to a marriage. Even couples in ideal circumstances need these, so how much more do you and your spouse need them, given the added pressure of travel?

Love, Roadwarrior@aol.com

Don't forget the advantages of using e-mail if you have a laptop computer that can communicate with your home computer. This is a way to stay in touch with great frequency and low expense. Be creative! Be open! If you're feeling lonely, share your feelings and needs with your spouse, so that he or she can understand and respond in ways that encourage you and keep you going.

Bill Hendricks

The tragedy is that many couples affected by business travel develop a grass-is-greener-on-the-other-side mentality. A spouse at home can be thinking, "He gets to leave town and stay in a nice hotel room and eat fancy dinners. But I'm stuck here with the usual problems!" Meanwhile, the traveler can be thinking, "She gets to have the house all to herself and maintain her routine. I have to disrupt my life and fly halfway across the country to sleep in a lousy hotel bed and work like the dickens all the time I'm gone!" Needless to say, it's hard to be a cheerleader with such a mind-set.

So may we admonish you as a marriage partner to try looking at things from your spouse's side of the fence? This is not to diminish your perspective. But for instance, if you are a wife who feels stuck at home, could you pause to consider the unique strain business travel puts on your husband? Consider that his employer is investing considerable dollars in both known and hidden costs to send him wherever he is going. In exchange, your husband is expected to produce results, far more than if he were staying in town. That's one reason why travelers invariably put in longer hours on the road than they do at their home base. There's a sense that they need to make the absolute most of the time.

But with these heightened expectations comes heightened anxiety. With each trip, the traveler must prove himself once again. And if your husband struggles with low self-esteem—as men commonly do, according to renowned marriage counselor Willard Harley—he will be highly sensitive to criticism and rejection. Unfortunately, business travel is a road strewn with land mines of criticism and rejection. Thus, if the deal falls through, if the customer says no, if headquarters calls and berates him for how things are turning out, if he gets bumped from a flight—he can feel mighty beat up emotionally.

According to Harley, what a man most needs in the midst of those downers is his wife's affirmation. He thrives on it. "Behind *every* man should be an admiring wife," Harley writes. "Biographies of great men prove it, and lives of all men show it: A man simply thrives on a woman's admiration. To a great extent men owe gratitude to their wives for this kind of emotional support, for without it, their confidence—the major source of their success—erodes and eventually crumbles" (*His Needs, Her Needs*, p. 153).

But now let's hop the fence and look at the other side. If you are a husband who is frequently on the road, have you stopped to consider the load you are dumping on your wife every time you leave town? All the responsibility falls on her. True, she doesn't have to put up with you. But then again, she has to put up with everything else, only now without your help. For many women, this can be a severe challenge; for some, it can feel overwhelming.

But no one can help your wife rise to that challenge nearly as well as you, her husband. You can do it even though you are miles away. The key, to return to Willard Harley, is affection. "To most women, affection symbolizes security, protection, comfort, and approval, vitally important commodities in their eyes. When a husband shows his wife affection, he sends the following messages: (1) I'll take care of you and protect you. You are important to me, and I don't want anything to happen to you. (2) I'm concerned about the problems you face, and I am with you. (3) I think you've done a good job, and I'm so proud of you" (p. 29).

"But how can I show my wife affection when I'm not there?" you may be asking. Well, now you can see the importance of remembering to get that leak in the tire fixed before you leave . . . of making a point to copy down your flight number and other particulars of your trip . . . of going over the schedule for what your wife hopes to accomplish while you are gone . . . of finding the time to call home and share a little "love on the phone." These things are practical expressions of affection. They provide some significant "hugs" when you can't be there to embrace your wife.

Significantly, Harley adds this anecdote about his wife, Joyce: "When I go on a trip, I often find little notes Joyce has packed among my clothes. She is telling me she loves me, of course, but the notes send another message as well. Joyce would like to get the same little notes from me, and I have tried to leave such notes behind—on her pillow, for example—when I go out of town" (p. 31).

Gentlemen, start your notepads! Your wife is longing to be embraced by your love. Don't let a silly thing like a business trip deprive her of that!

We've dwelled on homebound wives and traveling husbands because statistically they typify couples affected by travel. Obvi-

Just in Case

One way to head off a sense of isolation for a spouse at home is to leave a list of emergency numbers for various situations. Knowing where to turn for help, he or she won't feel stranded if there's a problem. (For more on planning, see chapter 8.)

ously, there are other combinations: homebound husbands with wives who must travel, marriages in which both partners travel, families that are on the road together as a family, and perhaps other arrangements.

The key is to realize that whatever problems travel creates for you, your spouse has needs as well. Thus, you'll want to become a champion for your mate, bombarding him or her with endless messages of support and encouragement. Travel or not, married partners need each other on their team, not on their backs.

Guard against Violating Your Partner's Trust

It goes without saying that loneliness places you at heightened risk for becoming unfaithful to your spouse. Legion are the stories of philandering husbands who, when forced to confess all, have admitted, "I was lonely out there on the road. Incredibly lonely. It was a strange city, and I didn't know anyone, so I was really vulnerable." Likewise, a wife who has been running around on her husband while he is away will say, "I needed someone to pay attention to me. That house gets awfully quiet when you're the only one there."

Let's be clear: Loneliness is no excuse for infidelity. When a man and a woman stand at the altar and recite their wedding vows, pledging to "forsake all others" and to be faithful to their mate "until death do us part," they do not add "unless, of course, we start feeling lonely." Actually, it's precisely because of things like loneliness—along with sickness, poverty, temptation, and other challenges—that couples need to commit themselves by reciting vows. It is crucial that a man and a woman state clearly and unequivocally at the start of their marriage that they can be counted on, that when trouble strikes—or conversely, when something "better" comes along—they will be found worthy of the trust their partner has placed in them.

Having said that, let's also affirm that unchecked loneliness provides fertile ground for the seeds of adultery. Thus, the wayward partner who says "I was lonely" has a point. Clearly, his or her legitimate needs for companionship, affection, and intimacy were somehow not being met.

That being the case, it seems obvious that loneliness is not something to be trifled with. Yet how many partners do exactly that by putting themselves in situations they know could lead to compromise? For example, Bill once knew a man who was struggling in his marriage. Things were far from hopeless, but there were plenty of issues that needed to be dealt with. Bill happened to meet this man over lunch at a convention. At the conclusion of the meal, the man agreed to furnish Bill with some printed information related to a product he was showing.

"Should I come by your booth?" Bill offered.

"No, just call my secretary," the man replied.

"You mean have her send it to me?"

"No, no," the man explained, "she's here. I brought her with me. Just call her room." And with that, he left.

Somehow, that didn't sound quite right to Bill. Not that it was wrong—just risky. In fact, it was incredibly foolish, given the man's situation. His marriage needed major repairs, yet here he was on the other side of the country, accompanied by a young, attractive woman who happened to be staying in the same hotel. Did he *want* to break up his marriage? Apparently, because within the year, Bill learned that the man's wife had filed for divorce. One reason why? You guessed it! The man had become involved with his secretary.

In contrast to this fellow, Bill has another friend who recently told him, "I had one close call early in my career. I almost had an affair with a woman I met on a trip. It scared me so badly that I've now set a policy for myself that I never travel unless my wife can go with me, or else another man in my company."

"Sounds expensive," Bill remarked.

"Yeah," he replied, "but how expensive is the alternative? I look at it as insurance."

Obviously, that solution won't work for everyone. But the lesson is that this man has actively taken steps to keep loneliness and its temptations at bay. He knows himself and his limitations, and he's choosing to steer clear of trouble.

One other point needs to be made. Earlier, we talked about the importance of friendships in dispelling loneliness. We must sound a note of caution, however, when the friendship is with someone of the opposite sex.

This has always been an issue for home-based spouses. It is increasingly an issue for spouses on the road. Some estimates predict that by the turn of the century, half of all business travelers will be women. That suggests there will be more situations in which men and women will be working together on the road and, naturally, building close friendships as a result. Nothing wrong with that! But let's be honest—it certainly raises the potential for violations of the marital bond.

"Oh, don't be so prudish!" someone will say.

To which we reply, Don't be so Pollyannish! When you're on the road, working long hours side by side with someone, you tend to develop a measure of trust and intimacy with that person. If your companion is a member of the opposite sex, the relationship can be quite platonic and innocent. But suppose you start feeling lonely or sad. Perhaps things at home aren't all they could be. Suddenly you can start looking to that other person for more than work-related support. You can start looking for emotional support as well.

And why not? Here's someone with whom you already have a great deal in common. You're sharing the experience of the trip. You're working together as a team. You're engaged in a common cause. Under these circumstances, it doesn't always happen but it *can* happen that you start seeing this other person as more than a coworker; you start seeing him or her as a co*partner* in a relational and emotional sense. You start noticing how attractive he or she suddenly seems, how witty, how brilliant, how confident, how understanding . . . *how desirable!*

We'll say more about sexual temptation in chapter 10. For now, it's enough to offer the warning that if we don't address our lonely feelings and seek healthy ways to meet our needs when travel separates us from our spouse, we are just asking for trouble. Loneliness may be an odd reassurance that we do, after all, need our mate, but it is a dangerous emotion to leave unchecked. Seriously lonely people become desperate people who do foolish things. If you see yourself on the edge, take action! *Use* your loneliness to drive you *toward* your partner—not away from him or her.

Stay Productive

Don't just stay active—be *productive!* Don't just do something—*accomplish* something! People sometimes say that the way to conquer loneliness is to stay busy. But being busy does not necessarily burn up the emotional tension that lies at the heart of loneliness. Instead, what is needed is a sense of purpose. So do things not just to pass the time but to have a life.

Can we be straightforward? If your life feels meaningful only when you are around your spouse, it's obvious why you feel so much tension and anxiety whenever you're apart: You're basing your life on your partner, and that is a shaky foundation. Living that way is not healthy. You can have a much richer life and a far more satisfying marriage if you will cultivate your own sense of yourself, apart from your wife or husband. Acknowledge and build on your God-given strengths and individuality. That's the way to bring value and significance to your world.

For example, Shirlene realized that every time her husband, Leonard, went out on duty as a member of the navy, she started coming apart emotionally. She felt aimless, lacking in direction. She'd end up spending hours in front of the TV, bored yet always with a nagging sense of worry. Then it dawned on her that this was the way life was going to be as the wife of a sailor.

So Shirlene thought about her options. She could stay where she was—wasting time. But she knew that would eventually lead to trouble. She could leave Leonard, but that would do no good. Finally, she determined to create her own set of activities, based on what was important to her. She joined the choir at the navy base chapel. She started taking piano lessons, something she'd always wanted to do. Once a week, she baked four loaves of bread—two for herself and two for a nearby senior center. She had a friend teach her how to maintain her car. And she planted a garden.

There were countless other ways in which Shirlene made a life for herself. The point is, she stopped wrapping her life around Leonard and started taking responsibility for herself. As a result, when Leonard came home on leave, he couldn't believe the change in her. She was much happier than she'd ever been. And he was never so delighted to be home. In fact, it was much harder for him to leave the next time. And after he did ship out, Shirlene noticed he was writing her more frequently.

Pay Attention to Chronic, Deep-Seated Loneliness

Loneliness is a normal response when travel separates you from your spouse. But for some people, the emotion goes beyond the normal to the abnormal. It so dominates their lives that they can hardly function. If this is the case for you, we want to point out that chronic loneliness is a serious condition that ought to be treated by a professional.

And we should also point out that if you are a frequent traveler whose homebound spouse is plagued by debilitating bouts of loneliness and depression whenever you are away, love demands that you pay attention to that. There may be issues involved that have nothing to do with your travel. But it's also possible that travel may be unhealthy for your marriage because it is incompatible with your spouse.

Recognizing that may lead to some hard choices. But in our opinion, signing up for an occupation that requires travel demands that you ask yourself two questions: (1) Do *I* have the right bent for being on the road; and (2) Does *my spouse* have a bent for having me on the road? Business travel affects your family every bit as much as it affects you. Thus, it is simply unfair and unloving not to allow the members of your family, who feel the impact of that travel, to have a say in deciding what is best.

None of us likes to feel lonely. But for most of us, loneliness is an inescapable by-product of business travel, both for those on the road and for those at home. So if there's no way around this feeling, is there a way to get through it? Yes: *strong love.*

Bruce Larsen observes, "Life breaks down not so much because of the terrible things that happen to us. Life breaks down because so few good things have happened to us. Just a few along the way can be like branches we can cling to as we climb up a mountain trail. No matter how steep the ascent, we can make it, if from time to time along the trail someone communicates to us that he or she loves us and therefore we are important" (*There's a Lot More to Health Than Not Being Sick,* p. 104).

When's the last time you communicated your love to your spouse?

7

All's Fair in Love and Travel

Conflict Resolution

*T*hey faced each other like a dog and a cat squaring off in an alley. He was snarling with anger; she was spitting mad. His jaw was locked in tension; her eyes were ablaze. Neither had any intention of backing down, yet they had reached an impasse. Who would make the next move?

He would. Calculating that now was the time to unleash one of his most potent weapons—an explosive insult gift-wrapped as a compliment—he calmly said, "I can't believe God would make someone so beautiful so stupid." Then he smiled, expecting to see her blown away by his sarcastic wit.

But the package failed to detonate. For without a moment's hesitation, she disarmed his little bomb by retorting, "I'm sure God had his reasons! He probably made me beautiful so you would love me, and he probably made me stupid so I could love you!"

Touché!

For as long as there have been couples, there have been conflicts. Some couples, like this one, fight their battles openly, producing lots of heat and sparks. Some fight more subtly, employing snide remarks and well-timed discourtesies. Others wage wars

of attrition, wearing each other down over time with silent pun-
ishment and passive-aggressive strategies. Some fight clean, others dirty. Some use the energy of conflict to strengthen their relationship; others use it to tear the marriage down.

But whatever style they use, *all* married couples experience conflict sooner or later. It's just a fact of life. So the issue is not how
to avoid conflict but what to do with it when it comes.

It certainly comes with travel. Just ask Jerry and Shawna.

Who Has It Harder?

Jerry is stretched out across his bed, watching *Monday Night
Football.* Shawna walks in and drops a load of laundry beside him.
She sits down and begins folding clothes.

"Kids down?" Jerry asks, sipping at a glass. Shawna nods.

The game continues. Presently Jerry grabs for a bowl of popcorn
on his pillow. "Want some popcorn?" he asks. Shawna shakes her
head and then notices him wiping his hands on the bedspread.

"Jerry!" she scolds. "You're getting butter all over the bedspread!
And look—you've got popcorn all over the bed!"

He looks down and picks up the larger kernels, then wipes the
smaller crumbs onto the floor.

"Don't just throw it on the rug! Now I have to vacuum again!"

"All right, all right! I'll get the Dust Buster and clean it up at
halftime."

"That'll be a first!" Shawna mutters to herself.

"What?" Jerry asks. Anger fills his face.

Shawna says nothing for a moment and then looks him in the
eye. "I said, 'That'll be a first,' Jerry! You never do the vacuuming.
I always do it."

"Yeah, well, I do my share of stuff, too."

"You do? Like what? It sccms to me that every time I get back
from a trip, I walk in the house and there's your socks to be picked
up and there's your shirts to be ironed and there's your glass or
there's your crumbs that you've left on the table! Once, just once,
I'd like to come in and not have to clean up after you!"

"Hey, look! I don't know what your problem is tonight. Maybe
you're still unwinding from your trade show. But I want you to

know that I do my chores just like you! I mow the yard and keep the cars up and write the checks. And remember, I take care of the kids while you're gone, and then I go and bust my butt at work, too! I work hard every day, and I don't get to travel, the way you do. So don't give me this you-never-do-*anything* bull!"

Shawna rolls her eyes. "Oh, here we go again about how I 'get' to travel, while you have it so tough! Do you think I'm on a vacation out there? You try standing in a convention hall for eight or ten hours a day, talking nonstop with total strangers. I'd like to see how you feel after two or three days of that—and then have to come home and clean up everything from while you were gone, *plus* start cooking meals again and bathing kids and doing laundry and ironing and all. It must be nice for you when I come back, so you can come home and sit back and watch TV!"

"Oh, brother!" Jerry is shaking his head in disgust. "So what do you want? You want to quit your job? Is that what you're saying?"

"No, I don't want to quit my job! I'm just asking for a little respect for what I do—and a little more help while I'm off doing it!"

"Well, you know," Jerry begins to say somewhat sarcastically, "you might just get a little more help if you'd ask for it a little nicer!" He pauses. "And I'd respect your job a lot more if instead of griping about how you do everything, you'd see that *both* of us do a lot—and I have a right to relax, just like you do."

"Then enjoy your stupid game!" Shawna says, storming out of the room with tears in her eyes.

The next morning, she and Jerry will have calmed down, and the routine of day-to-day life will return. But a question mark hangs over the long-term prospects for their marriage. Will the issues and tensions that surface in arguments like this ever be dealt with openly and resolved? Or will the marriage slowly erode as it's hammered by wave upon wave of conflict in which the point seems to be to prevail rather than to communicate?

Are You Overdrawn at the Love Bank?

It would seem to be self-evident why conflict resolution is such an important part of marriage. Yet as Jerry and Shawna illustrate, for many couples the only thing that is self-evident is the inevitability of conflict—not the fact that couples must work through their differences if they want their marriages to thrive. In other words, too many couples assume that spats are part of the marriage contract. "Jerry's just a jerk sometimes," Shawna will say matter-of-factly. Likewise, Jerry takes it for granted that "when Shawna gets home, it usually takes her a couple of days to get off her high horse."

Attitudes like these are quite common. But they betray an unfortunate belief about the marriage relationship—that it is basically a war between a man and a woman, occasionally interrupted by a truce. As Dr. Tony Evans puts it, "Some people may get married by a justice of the peace, but it doesn't take long before it looks like they were wed by the secretary of war."

In fact, even when peace breaks out and tokens of love are shown, some couples continue their mistrust. They keep up their guard, each spouse suspicious of how the other might be taking advantage of him or her during moments of relative calm.

For example, when Shawna brings home from the road some gift for Jerry, he is liable to think, "What's she getting ready to ask me for now?" Conversely, when Shawna comes home and finds the kitchen clean, the floors swept, and the garbage taken out, she is liable to call her mother and say, "Guess what! Jerry cleaned the house while I was gone. I'm sure he'll be running off to play golf tomorrow."

These are sad words, because they reveal a negative attitude toward the relationship. What a miserable way to go through life! Perhaps that's why about half of all marriages end in divorce—and who can say how many of the rest are genuinely satisfying to both parties?

Unresolved conflict acts like acid on a marriage relationship. It eats away at trust and loyalty. And remember, without those, you don't really have a relationship.

Willard Harley illustrates this corrosive tendency by suggesting that every person figuratively has what he calls a "love bank." When a married person has a positive interaction with his or her spouse, a certain number of "love units" are deposited in that spouse's account. When the interaction is negative, love units are withdrawn. It's easy to see how constant conflict that never gets resolved can quickly lead to a couple being overdrawn!

Yet a lot of us are living on "spousal credit," aren't we? We are deep in relational debt because, quite frankly, we make ourselves awfully hard to live with. It's not that we find ourselves in disagreement with our partner—that's unavoidable! It's that in those disagreements, we are *disagreeable.* Our spouse has little chance of working through conflict with us, because we're not interested in working through it. We're more concerned with winning the argument and getting our way.

Harley and others have developed some excellent resources for turning this situation around—*for those who want to.* If you are experiencing a lot of conflict in your marriage and want to start dealing with it constructively, we urge you to get ahold of some of those materials.

By the way, resolving conflicts with your spouse affects more than just the home front. Studies have shown that marital discord has a profound—and costly—effect on your performance in the workplace. For example, a 1995 report by the Conference Board estimated that personal concerns, including marital and family difficulties, cost American businesses $200 billion annually.

Jim's experience as a corporate chaplain certainly corroborates this finding. After years of counseling employees and their spouses, he has observed that marital conflict is a major demotivating factor in work. About half of his counseling time is devoted to people struggling significantly in their marriages. These individuals invariably lose effectiveness on the job because of their conflicts at home. Time spent in Jim's office; time spent in further counseling with outside professionals; distracting phone calls; an excessive number of personal days taken; lack of focus and energy—it all adds up.

So if you and your spouse fail to work through your differences at home, it may prove expensive for your employer. It may also prove expensive for the two of you. In fact, you might just find yourself looking for a new job because your employer has determined that replacing you—a costly proposition in itself—is less expensive than putting up with your personal difficulties.

Of course, this relationship between home and work operates the other way, too: Troubles at work can create conflicts at home.

One survey of employees at IBM revealed that 25 percent admitted that family-related problems resulted from their travel. American Express uncovered similar tension in a more dramatic way. When the company scheduled an out-of-town department conference during a Halloween weekend, 16 percent of those who were supposed to go refused, citing conflicts with children's activities ("Work and Family," *Wall Street Journal*, Nov. 9, 1992, p. B2).

Obviously, not all of us are in a position to say no to our employer's demands. Many of us have little choice but to comply, even if it means disappointment and anger for ourselves and our family. Either way, if we feel stress on the job, we're liable to take things out on our family. We don't always mean to, but we do. And one of the most common ways in which work can affect the conflicts in our family is through business travel.

Four Connections between Travel and Conflict

We have already said that conflict is an inevitable part of marriage. Couples will have disagreements whether or not one or both of them travel on business. But in our experience, business travel has some interesting connections to marital conflict.

1. Travel Can Cause Conflict

In the case of Jerry and Shawna, Jerry has come to resent Shawna's travel. He doesn't explain exactly why he feels that way, but it is evident from his comments.

Other couples experience conflict because of the way travel imposes on the marriage relationship. It disrupts communication. It creates a climate for loneliness. It interferes with a couple's sex life. It may complicate the finances. Thus, as it affects area after area, travel itself can become a hassle. Indeed, some couples end up angrier at the travel than they do at each other. They see it as a necessary evil they would just as soon do without.

2. Travel Can Aggravate Existing Conflict

Neil and Trudy were having a hard time conceiving, and in the middle of an argument over this problem, Trudy blurted out, "Well,

87

if you were home more, maybe I'd have half a chance of getting pregnant!"

The resentment toward travel is obvious. Yet what was the real issue here? Not travel, but the frustration of not having a baby. Thus, when Neil defended himself by saying he was only trying to provide security for Trudy and his family-to-be, he was off on a rabbit trail. He was sincere, and what he was saying was true. But financial security was not the point. The argument was not about whether he was providing for the family or whether travel was required to do that. Not getting pregnant was the real source of the conflict.

3. Travel Can Be an Escape from Conflict

Husbands are notorious for walking away from a shouting match with their wives, getting in the car or on a plane, and taking off with the attitude, "Oh, well, I'll be gone for a few days, and she'll calm down. She'll get over it." But that only creates resentment and causes the wife to lose respect for her husband. Why? Because it minimizes her feelings and leaves her in the lurch. She feels treated like a non-person, as if her needs and concerns don't matter.

It's a sad thing, but we know people who are on the road more than they are home because they are avoiding pain and problems in their family relationships. For example, there's the father who feels intense pain about his troubled teenager. There's the wife who longs to get away from her alcoholic husband. There's the man who doesn't know what to do about his aged, infirm mother, who has become so demanding. These people may rack up countless frequent flyer miles and log endless days on the road, not because they enjoy it out there or need to be out there, but because out there they don't have to face reality back at the ranch.

If that describes you, may we speak bluntly? By staying out of the line of fire, you are practicing a form of denial. You are pretending that the conflict doesn't exist. You think that by ignoring it, the problem will go away, or at least you won't have to deal with it.

But three facts remain: (1) The problem *is there*; it hasn't gone away; it does exist; (2) you may be able to escape the immediate conflict, but you cannot escape the *emotional impact* of that conflict on you (which explains why many businesspeople who use travel as an escape fight problems such as substance abuse, pornography, and psychosomatic ailments); (3) *someone* is having to deal with the mess at home. So at some point you have to ask yourself, Am I being fair by pushing off this pain, this trouble, onto someone else? Wouldn't it be healthier and more responsible to face it squarely, as tough as that may be?

4. Travel Can Prevent Conflict Resolution

Conflict resolution is a matter of communication. Obviously, if you are not home to work out differences with your spouse, it is unlikely they will be worked out. Travel tends to prevent you from resolving conflicts. It's not that you can't pick up the phone, call your mate, and say, "Look, I spoke out of turn. I was wrong. I apologize. Let's try to work this out." But realistically, that's hard to do.

It's a lot harder than if you and your partner are home for dinner, and you don't want to eat with a lot of tension in the air. In that case, you can sit down and talk things through. But if you are on the road? It's just easier to let the conflict ride. "I'll wait until I get back home," a traveler will say. Or the home-based spouse may think, "My honey is busy with the trip. I'll wait until he or she is back to bring this up again." Sometimes that may be the wiser policy. Still, how does it affect the relationship to have turmoil festering while the traveler is away?

However, there's a more subtle aspect to this issue. When a couple has been fighting and travel takes them apart, time and distance have a way of promoting reflection on the conflict. For example, a traveler may be sitting in a plane or a hotel room and suddenly start thinking things over. Now detached from the heat of battle, he or she may be able to see the conflict from a fresh perspective. Perhaps there is insight, a new sense of empathy with his or her spouse, maybe even remorse. In short, the traveler can become remarkably pliable and reasonable, and it seems certain that things can be worked out once the traveler gets home.

Yet what happens when the traveler rejoins his or her spouse? Oftentimes nothing happens! Somehow, all of that insight and good feeling and sanity can evaporate (especially if there's been a rocky re-entry, as described in chapter 13). The traveler, so considerate and constructive in his or her thoughts on the road, suddenly retreats back to the old posture of defensiveness, and the conflict rages on. Who can say why this happens? The point is that it does happen, and in this way travel can become a hindrance to resolving conflict. For it doesn't really matter what you say to the spouse in your head—it's the spouse in your house that you've got to deal with!

Pursuing Fusion, Not Fission

Probably all of us have seen pictures of the mushroom cloud created by a thermonuclear explosion. It's a graphic reminder of the awesome energy released when a hydrogen atom is split—a process known as nuclear fission.

Another way to create energy—at least in theory—is to *fuse* two atoms together. In fact, this method is superior to fission because it not only yields a tremendous amount of energy, it creates no hazardous by-products.

When it comes to conflicts in marriage, we need a lot more fusion and less fission. Too many homes today have a toxic little mushroom cloud boiling up from inside because the couples that live there are tearing each other apart. Their spats produce lots of energy, but they are destructive and leave aftereffects that are lethal to the relationship.

How much better it would be if married partners would use the heat of the moment to fuse their lives together! In physics, there is great debate as to whether fusion is possible, but in marriage, it *can* happen. A couple can resolve their differences in ways that energize the relationship.

We've already alluded to the many fine resources available that explain the "technology" of conflict resolution. Here are some suggestions related to conflict resolution and travel, beginning with the obvious.

Marriage expert Norm Wright offers some good advice on how to have a fair argument with your spouse. He recommends a process for expressing your feelings openly and honestly without diminishing the value or self-esteem of your partner.

There are five basic ways of dealing with marital conflict: yield, resolve, win, withdraw, compromise.

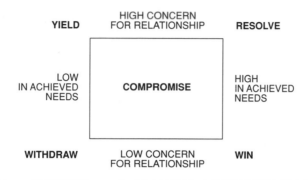

The upper bar of the box represents a high concern for the relationship, while the lower bar represents a low concern. The left bar represents a low concern for achieved needs, while the right bar represents a high concern. *Withdrawing* and *winning* are the least helpful mechanisms for strengthening your marriage; *yielding* or *resolving* are the best strategies, with *compromise* being a cross section of the two, less helpful but also less harmful.

Withdrawing allows you to get out of conflict quickly, but your needs are not met. *Winning* may allow you to achieve success in fulfilling your needs or establishing your opinion, but it does little in the way of supporting your spouse. On the other hand, *yielding* may not allow you to have your needs met, but typically it does enable you to support the needs of your spouse and typically is done with the full understanding of the trade-off between your needs and your spouse's. *Resolution* is the highest form of conflict achievement and, since it considers the viewpoint of

(continued)

each individual, establishes the best solution for the needs of the marriage. However, it takes the most work. *Compromise,* obviously, is the situation in which both parties get a little something and lose a little something. However, some measure of peace is re-established in the relationship.

You can evaluate this approach for yourself, but chances are you will agree that the higher your concern for the relationship, the more likely you are to work in the upper quadrants of Dr. Wright's diagram. And if you find you are living in the lower quadrants but would like to show a higher regard for your spouse, our suggestion is to begin exercising the marriage-building techniques in Wright's book (Norm Wright, *The Pillars of Marriage,* pp. 146–60; see also Philip Yancey, *Care-Fronting*).

Have Your Conflicts!

The only way to resolve conflict is to *have* conflict. So go ahead—get it out and fight it out! Put the issues on the table and have at it. Let your thoughts and feelings be known. Honor each other by sharing your honest opinions about the matter at hand. You are going to deal with the conflict one way or another, so you might as well do it up front, in a straightforward, "clean" way.

Actually, this approach to conflict may look and feel messy, especially if you are of a temperament that shies away from conflict or if you come from a background in which conflicts were never dealt with openly. But realize that it is preferable to get "down and dirty" honest and then clean things up rather than to try to keep everything nice and pleasant and allow the dirt to accumulate inside.

Pay Attention to Timing

It's said that timing is everything, and travel definitely introduces some timing considerations. For example, the re-entry period is not the best time to try to work out a major disagreement.

Here's a husband getting off a plane, and boy, is his wife steamed! He didn't get the car serviced before he left town like he was supposed to, and sure enough, it broke down on her. She has spent the afternoon sitting in the waiting room of a repair shop, and she used that time to compose a splendid speech that will give her husband what for.

But is the airport terminal the best place for her to get into this problem? She's got a legitimate beef, no doubt about it. But given the timing, that conflict is liable to escalate unnecessarily. It might be more productive to wait until her husband catches his breath, off-loads some of the stress of his travel, and is in a frame of mind to even hear what she has to say.

A similarly poor choice of timing for dealing with conflict is the day of departure. Sometimes this is unavoidable (see chapter 12). But wading into a muddy issue just as the traveler is getting ready to leave is like shouting just as he or she serves a tennis ball or starts a golf swing.

If you and your partner find yourselves getting into a problem area just as the taxi is pulling up, we suggest you agree together to postpone the discussion until a more suitable time. It may be after the traveler has arrived at his or her destination, or maybe even after the trip. But by putting the item on the agenda for future consideration, you avoid rushing through it and handling it badly.

Don't Blame Your Conflicts on Travel

As noted above, travel creates conflicts of its own, but oftentimes travel is not the problem. So what is the problem? In resolving conflict, it helps to be clear as to exactly what the root of the trouble is.

By the way, this is a good time to mention that there are in fact some *benefits* to business travel. For one thing, it is part of the work that provides a living for your family. Travel means the opportunity to broaden your knowledge and experience, to meet new people, to expand your perspective of the world. Travel allows your spouse at home a measure of independence and freedom. And if your relationship is reasonably healthy, travel can re-energize affection and cause you both to look forward to enjoying each other's company.

Other positives could be mentioned. The point is that while travel certainly imposes on a relationship, it alone does not have the power to hurt a relationship. Thus, a couple is usually mistaken if they lay all the blame for their marital problems on travel. In all likelihood, the source of their troubles lies elsewhere.

Change What You Can, Accept What You Can't

When we say that the goal in dealing with conflict is to achieve some sort of resolution, it's important to understand that resolution does not mean perfection. Sometimes "working things out" means they are only partially worked out. Maybe not all needs can be satisfied. Maybe there's compromise that goes hand in hand with a bit of disappointment.

Another way of saying it is that marriage is all about two less-than-perfect people learning to live together in less-than-perfect harmony—but harmony nonetheless. What's more, they have to do so in a less-than-perfect world. Jim recently witnessed a dramatic illustration of this reality. A couple he knows has had to deal with one of the most tragic situations any family can face: the accidental death of their twenty-month-old child.

The incident occurred as the parents were preparing for a vacation. The mother needed to run a last-minute errand, so she hopped in the car and began backing out of the driveway. Little did she realize that her toddler had somehow got out of the house and wandered into the path of the car. The child was killed instantly, to the mother's utter horror.

What an unspeakable tragedy! Can you imagine the potential for conflict in that home? Experts say that the untimely death of a child, whatever the circumstances, typically fills parents with guilt and shame, which often lead to the parents blaming one another. Not surprisingly, a majority of marriages that undergo such incredible stress end in divorce shortly thereafter.

Thus it is remarkable that this couple has largely managed to get beyond the blaming stage as well as the guilt of this incident. With great courage, they have sought ways to value, affirm, accept, forgive, and love each other, even as they grieve their loss openly. They cannot change what happened. Nor can they soon escape their disappointment and feelings of irretrievable loss. They will live with that pain for some time to come. Nevertheless, they have

94

determined to let this tragedy fuse their lives together. What an inspiration to us all!

When Things Are out of Control, Seek Help

Our first suggestion was to face conflict head-on. However, we feel a bit of trepidation in offering the advice to "get it out and fight it out." This counsel is fine for couples who are relatively healthy emotionally. But what if you or your spouse is emotionally unhealthy? We certainly don't want to encourage any sort of emotional or physical abuse.

Every reader must take responsibility for how he or she deals with the conflicts in his or her marriage. But if your relationship is marked by behaviors such as violence, prolonged bouts of shouting and name-calling, relentless verbal attacks that create hurt and pain, or by one of the partners drifting into long periods of withdrawal and deep depression, then you need to seek the help of a professional marriage counselor. Something is amiss, and it is unlikely that trying to "fight it out" is going to do much good. Indeed, it is liable to do more harm than good.

Arguments that escalate into abuse and violence are terrible things, not least for the fact that they damage common perceptions about conflict. They cause many people to fear conflict instead of accepting it as a part of life and using it to strengthen their relationships. In the end, that's what you and your spouse will want to do: Face the disagreements as they come, air them out, listen carefully to each other, and work together to find solutions that satisfy your needs.

Perhaps it would help to recall that the person you married was the one you initially valued so much that you vowed to "forsake all others, to have and to hold, and to love in sickness and in health, in riches and in poverty, till death do you part." If you can reclaim that perspective, it will help frame your conflicts with hope. And hope will give you long-term determination to work toward a mutually satisfying relationship, as well as short-term motivation to resolve irritating tensions. The long view says that your marriage is worth fighting for, not fighting over.

Who's Running This Railroad, Anyway?

Planning and Scheduling

*I*n the heyday of the railroads, conductors kept their trains running on time by glancing at a trusty pocket watch. Today, it takes esoteric math and state-of-the-art computers to keep the world's railroads, airlines, and other transportation systems in sync. Even with all that, a couple of hours of bad weather at a strategic point is all it takes to throw even the most sophisticated projections out of whack and cause travel delays from coast to coast.

Sometimes it seems that way in marriage and family life, too. For many of us, life has become hopelessly complicated. We have to spend more and more time figuring out how to organize our time. Then, despite our best efforts to balance all the demands, it only takes an unexpected curve ball—the complications that often occur with business travel—to really throw us for a loop.

Business travel intrudes on many aspects of the home, but perhaps none is more affected than the family schedule. Each of us has certain needs and expectations that demand a certain amount of *time*. Travel is a master thief of time—unless we take preventive measures. Unfortunately, many travelers and their spouses leave the door wide open to trouble, as the following incident illustrates.

The Weekend

Colleen is standing at a pay phone in Salt Lake City. It's Friday afternoon, and she's just learned that her flight home to San Diego has been cancelled. The airline has rescheduled her on another carrier, so she's calling her husband, Brandon, to let him know. But the phone at the bait-and-tackle shop Brandon runs just rings and rings.

"Where the heck is he?" Colleen mutters to herself. "Brandon is *always* there on Friday afternoons!" Finally, she hangs up and calls home. No answer. Then she calls a marina near Brandon's store, but no one there knows where he is.

In desperation, Colleen calls Jack, Brandon's partner. "He must know what's up," she thinks. But Jack's phone is busy and stays that way for the next five minutes. By now, the flight is in its final boarding stage, and Colleen has to give up. She tries to call from the plane a couple of times, but there's still no answer at the bait shop or at home.

Not surprisingly, when Colleen finally arrives in San Diego, there is no Brandon to meet her at the airport. In fact, Brandon won't show up for another forty-five minutes—and since he doesn't know about the cancelled flight, he will go to the wrong gate! In the end, Brandon won't find Colleen until late that evening—after Colleen's been sitting for nearly two hours, fuming! Needless to say, their reunion that night is a little rocky!

Saturday is no better. Brandon announces at breakfast that he has plans to go sailing with Jack. Colleen reminds him that he promised to paint the room of their daughter, Nicole. "I'll be back this afternoon," he says. "I'll get started on it this evening."

"But Daddy," Nicole protests, "I've got a friend coming to spend the night!"

"Then I'll do it tomorrow."

"Oh, no you won't!" Colleen says. "Tomorrow is your uncle's birthday, and your mom has a big party planned, and I told her we'd be there!"

"You what?!" Brandon rolls his eyes. "I'm supposed to help Charlie work on his boat!"

"I thought you were going to paint Nicole's room."

"Look, I don't like you being away all week, and then when you come home, you suddenly start rearranging my schedule for me! I've had a hard week and I need a break and I'm going sailing!" With that, he grabs his gear and heads out the door.

"What about my room, Mom?" Nicole asks.

"I don't know, honey," Colleen replies, tears welling up in her eyes. "Ask your father when he comes home!"

The Necessity of Planning

Colleen and Brandon's household seems to operate according to the old saying that most of us don't plan to fail—we fail to plan! Is your family like that? If so, you can expect lots of conflict and misery every time a business trip comes along. Coordinating schedules to meet each family member's needs is tough enough without travel. It's that much more of a challenge when a business trip has to be factored in. And if everyone is going in different directions, unmindful of—or worse, unconcerned with—everyone else's plans and expectations, disaster awaits.

Planning and scheduling are crucial for a family because ultimately love is expressed as a function of time: To love each other means to spend time with each other and to respect each other's time.

Think back to the days when you and your spouse were courting. You probably planned your whole day around each other. You wanted to spend every moment you could in each other's presence. Why? Because you instinctively knew that *love* is spelled t-i-m-e.

Well, nothing has changed—at least, the nature of love has not changed. It is still a function of time. But has your love for each other changed? If so, that may be because over the years you have allowed increasing demands on your time to crowd out those moments with your partner that communicate, "I love you."

There's only one way to rebuild that love: *Make time for one another!*

"But guys," you may be saying, "we've got less time for each other now—especially with travel! How can you expect us to make more time for each other?"

Schedule it! Henry Kaiser said, "Determine what you want more than anything else in life, write it down, write down the means by which you intend to attain it, and permit nothing to deter you from pursuing it." Isn't that exactly what we would do to achieve a business goal? Then why not do it to pursue relational goals? Indeed, one of the most important means we have for building a strong marriage relationship is to write our spouses into our schedule.

We're not trying to lay a guilt trip on anyone. We and our wives and families struggle with this same issue of planning and scheduling. But one thing we know: It is absolutely certain that no relationship between two people grows apart due to spending meaningful time with one another and respecting each other's time. It's just a fact of our humanity.

So if we intend to make the most of our marriage and family life, we have to take planning seriously. There are so many things we could spend our time on! Even if we were single and "free" of family commitments, we could not do all there is to do in the world. There is no end of things we *could* do; many of us feel as if there were no end of things we *should* do. So we have to make choices. What are the choices we are willing to make for our loved ones?

Planning is about making choices. It's essentially like preparing a budget—except that when it comes to time, we all have a fixed amount to work with. However, for the business traveler, a great deal of that limited resource is devoted to being on the road, leaving the traveler less discretionary time to spend on the needs of his or her spouse or family.

What to do? We'll consider some strategies in a moment. But let's not jump ahead before we've gained an adequate appreciation for what is involved here. You're misreading us if you think we're saying that somehow you've got to cut back on your travel and spend more time at home if you want to preserve your marriage and family. For some, that may be the best thing that could happen. But that's not our primary concern.

Our point is that with or without travel, time is a fundamental fact of life, and the management of time is a fundamental challenge for the home. Travel tends to complicate the picture, but the question remains: How are we handling that challenge? First there's the matter of cultivating relationships by *being present* enough to connect with our spouse and other family members. Then there's the matter of *paying attention* to the scheduling needs of each member of the family. These two aspects of time management go hand in hand.

Missing the Band Concert

For example, here is a boy who comes home from school and sits down to supper. He notices that his father is absent, so he asks, "Where's Dad?"

"Oh, he had to go out of town tonight and tomorrow night," his mother replies.

"Does that mean he's going to miss my band concert tomorrow?" the boy asks.

"I guess so, honey. I'm sorry."

There are a lot of unknowns about this scenario, so we have to be careful about jumping to conclusions. But there are some ominous signs in what we do know. For one thing, why did the boy have to ask where his father was? Why did no one inform him as soon as possible that his father was called away? Furthermore, what consideration, if any, was given to the boy's expectation that his father would be at the band concert?

Again, there's a lot we don't know. But what we see here is the hint of a destructive pattern that is present in many a traveler's home. The issue is not just the traveler's absence—although sometimes the grief that results from this loss dominates all other feelings, as we saw in chapter 6. For this boy, however, two impressions are being formed that may have profound implications later in life. They are: (1) My father comes and goes and, it would appear, would just as soon be away from me as with me; (2) my schedule matters very little in the overall scheme of the family—it can be altered without notice or even ignored if need be.

Perhaps you think we're reading into things. Could be. But not if this scenario repeats itself again and again over the years as this boy is growing up. Boys (and girls) need their fathers, and based on the little we know, it would seem that this boy has very little of his father.

How could he have more of him, *even if his dad has to be away?* A little planning would help! For example, imagine the father sitting in his office in the middle of the day. The phone rings. "Jake, we've got a hot lead out in Amarillo! You need to go check it out!"

Okay, so Dad's going to have to leave town. He happens to be in a business in which that happens. He frequently has to drop everything and catch the next flight to go chase a prospect. Fair enough! But in leaving town, even on a moment's notice, is there any reason why he cannot consider the needs of his family? *If he's done his planning, he can!*

Let's say that as he hangs up the phone, this man—seasoned traveler that he is—puts into effect a little protocol he has developed. He calls it his dash plan: It's a checklist he goes through whenever he has to dash to the airport to catch a plane. One of the items on the list is to look over his appointment book for the days he'll be gone. He does so and notices that tomorrow night he was planning to attend his son's band concert. (This man was wise enough to write that commitment in his book. Unfortunately, too many fathers don't write such things down, which is why they find themselves missing a lot of their kids' activities.)

That immediately takes him to another item on his checklist: a call home. He has to make that call from his car, since he's dashing to the airport. As he discusses things with his wife, he says, "Honey, you know *I was planning* [Oh, those words are so important!] to go to Jimmy's band concert tomorrow night. Now I can't. Will you please tell him as soon as he gets home from school that I'm going to have to miss it and how disappointed I am? I really wanted to be there to hear him play."

This father can say those words because they're true (don't say them if they aren't true!). He really is disappointed. He really did want to be there, for his son's sake. By communicating that to his son—even secondhand—his son gets a part of his father; his dad is not completely absent. Sure, it's not as good as if Dad could have

101

been at the band concert. But at least he's not a no-show. The boy and his father can *share* the disappointment. The boy can deal with that. What he finds harder to deal with is if the disappointment is his alone.

But the father's dash plan doesn't stop there. The checklist calls for a phone call home at the earliest opportunity. He won't be able to call home that night. He'll be up until early in the morning, preparing to meet with his prospective client. So the earliest opportunity to call turns out to be at 7:12 A.M., exactly eight minutes before Jimmy's car pool will pick him up for school. Limited time? You bet! But the father makes the most of it, first by calling, then by giving his son his complete attention during the call.

When Jimmy gets on the line, his father says, "Hey, pal, I know you have to get off to school in a few minutes, so I guess we'll have to talk fast. I'm sorry I didn't get to say good-bye yesterday. Did Mom tell you I have to be away tonight?"

"Yeah, she did."

"It means I won't be at your band concert."

"I know."

"That really hurts! I hate to miss it. You've been practicing so hard! I was looking forward to hearing you with the whole band. Will you do me a favor?"

"What's that?"

"Will you give me a special, private concert when I get home?"

"Yeah, I guess. It won't be the same."

"No, it won't. It sure won't. Gosh, it kills me the way these trips come up! You know, I like what I do for a living, but man, it sure makes it hard to be a dad! Son, I love you. Do your best! I'll be home tomorrow."

Can you see what we mean when we say that love is largely a function of time? We may not have much time, thanks to travel. But love means, first of all, making the most of the time we do have with each other, even when that time is interrupted or limited; love also means respecting each other's time—that is, respecting each other's schedules.

Jimmy's father cannot be there for the concert. Under different circumstances, he might have been able to plan his trip around it. Nevertheless, he displays great respect for his son, and his son's interests, by communicating that the concert *matters*—that his son matters. His son's schedule is not just an afterthought, to be kept or not as circumstances dictate. His father demonstrates that he can be trusted to honor the events of Jimmy's life, even if he cannot always attend them. He shows respect for his son, which forms a foundation for love.

This story presents a relationship between a father and his son, but the same principles apply to other relationships in the home. Scheduling and planning matter because each person in the family, and his or her time, matters. It's important to say "I love you" to each other; planning specifies *when* that love will find expression, in the same way that a budget specifies *where* a family's money will go. Scheduling is a way of choosing to "spend time." It essentially says, for example, "On Saturday, right after lunch, out of all the myriad possibilities for what I could be doing, I'm going to paint my daughter's room. That's how I'm going to spend my time. It's on the schedule." Thus, by means of a schedule, "I love you" translates into "I will paint your room." Love is a function of time.

The Master Thief of Time

No doubt all of us would like to become better at using our time and better at planning our time in ways that improve our relationships. But as we've pointed out, business travel is a master at robbing us, as couples and families, of our time. It *steals* the amount of available time, and it *disrupts* the time we do have together.

But there is a more insidious way that travel intrudes on the family schedule. Travel tends to isolate the traveler from the rest of the family in such a way that the family begins to—often has to—schedule around the traveler and, eventually, without him or her. Thus, travel can introduce emotional distance as well as physical distance. Not only is the traveler not there in person, he or she is no longer there in spirit either. Thus, as the family budgets its time, the traveler can become ignored—which, again, means the person gets ignored.

This situation is to some extent unavoidable for travelers who must be away for extended periods of time, such as military per-

103

sonnel or businesspeople sent for several weeks or months on an overseas assignment. Obviously, the family has to get on with planning its day-to-day activities. It cannot allow the absence of the loved one to put everything on hold.

Even so, there is real danger when the traveler is dropped from the family's planning. Again, it creates emotional distance. If you are a home-based spouse, have you ever felt a sense of intrusion when your traveler returns from a trip? To some extent, that's normal. But it may also be a sign that his or her stake in the family's life is being allowed to slip a bit. Pay attention to that! You don't want the emotional distance to grow. You want to take steps to shrink it.

Of course, there is a flip side to all this: The traveler can make his own schedule so important that he expects everything in the family to revolve around his agenda. Jim knows someone whose father had this kind of egocentric mentality. Everything in that man's home had to revolve around his travel plans. If he was leaving for a trip in the morning, he demanded that his wife get up and make him breakfast prior to his departure—yes, even if it was 3:00 or 4:00 A.M! When he was coming home, he demanded that his family be at the airport to greet him. And if it was an evening arrival, dinner had to be waiting.

These rigid demands were this man's way of driving home the point that he was in charge of his household. By golly, he was the boss, and what mattered was *him!* As you can imagine, that attitude created lots of tension and turmoil in the family, in part because no one could make plans for fear of interfering with the father's plans. Everyone had to be "at attention," ready to salute the father's agenda.

This is an exaggerated case, to be sure. But it shows the extremes to which travelers can go when they think their travel plans are so important. Are they any more important than the plans of the rest of the family?

Certainly, the traveler has legitimate needs. But so do his or her spouse and the rest of the members of the family. Together, they must find ways to accommodate each other, and plan the family calendar accordingly. Thus, if you are the traveler, you are not free to ignore what is going on at home while you are away. A sixth-grade band concert may seem utterly inconsequential when you are thousands of miles away, negotiating a sale or making a presentation. Meanwhile, in an auditorium back home, that sale or presentation can seem like a big fat imposition to your child, who was hoping to show you how well he or she is doing in band. You may have no choice but to be out of town. Yet as we've seen, out of sight need not mean out of mind.

Some Pointers for Planning

Planning and scheduling are probably as much art as science. There are judgments to be made that reflect values and priorities. So there are no hard-and-fast, foolproof rules for scheduling your family's day-to-day activities. Even if there were, travel always finds a way to torpedo the "perfect plan." Still, there are some basic principles that can help your planning—and your life together—go a lot more smoothly. Here are a few suggestions.

Communicate Needs and Expectations

As always, good communication is the place to start. You can't plan for what you don't know about. Thus, it's crucial that family members be encouraged to express their needs and expectations whenever they need to—ideally, as soon as they become aware of them.

We saw an example of what *not* to do in the case of Brandon. He waited until Saturday morning to announce that he was going sailing that day. There's nothing wrong with sailing. But as Colleen pointed out, he had already indicated that he would paint his daughter's room on Saturday. Reneging on that commitment was bad enough. But even if Nicole's room had not needed painting, waiting until the last minute to inform the family of his plans was inexcusable because it gave no one else a chance to evaluate those plans in light of their own needs.

The only way a family can function as a team is if everyone keeps each other informed. Otherwise, you don't have a team— you have a mob! Everyone's doing his or her own thing, and no one's happy, because no one knows what to expect. The more sensible approach is to keep the lines of communication wide open!

One caveat on this point: If you have teenagers, they may not *want* to let anyone in on their plans. They may enjoy the idea that parents are not intruding on their agenda. That's an age characteristic, and something to be factored in. It means that many times they may show up at the last minute with a need for which they expect your help. You may or may not be able (or feel it is wise) to accommodate their request. But don't just give them a sermon on responsibility. Let them deal with the consequences of failing to make plans with others in mind. And of course, be a model of wise planning yourself.

Hold a Yearly Powwow

One way that we have found to help travel schedules at Interstate Battery is to hold an annual planning meeting during the first week of January. At that meeting, we identify key dates and projects for the coming year, as well as other matters relevant to our work. This allows us to prepare for them in advance.

Jim and Brenda hold a similar meeting at home. Then, by comparing the business and personal calendars, they find it easier to avoid conflicts. Obviously, they cannot anticipate events that are yet to be scheduled. But they can anticipate dates that are recurrent, like birthdays and anniversaries, or specially planned, like conventions and vacations.

Create a Master Calendar

To us, the suggestion to combine work and family planning on one calendar seems so obvious that we hesitate to include it, not wanting to insult anyone's intelligence. Yet time and again, we are amazed to discover families that have no overall calendar for scheduling activities that affect the family's life.

Too many families operate on separate tracks. The parents have their work schedules. The kids have their calendars for school.

The mothers (usually) keep some sort of record for family matters, such as Little League games, church picnics, and appointments with doctors and dentists. But this hodgepodge approach leaves a lot of cracks for things to fall through.

How many times has your family had a conversation like this one?

Daughter: "Mom, the soccer team is having an end-of-the-season party at Coach's lake house next week. Can I go?"

Mother: "Well, what day is it?"

Daughter: "Thursday afternoon."

Mother: "That's fine by me, but I have to work. How will you get home?"

Daughter: "I don't know. Dad, can you pick me up?"

Father: "Honey, I'm going to be out of town."

Mother: "I didn't know that! You didn't tell me about that!"

Father: "Sure I did. Remember last month, after the divisional meeting? I said I had to go up to headquarters next week."

Mother: "Well, sure, you said you had to go to headquarters. But you didn't specify this coming week!"

Father: "I'm sure I did. Well, anyway, I do."

Mother: "But we're supposed to meet with Al Jones about the taxes next week."

Father: "Who set that up?"

Mother: "I did! You told me to schedule a time with him."

Father: "Well, I wish you had checked with me. That's not going to work."

Mother: "Well, how was I to know you were going to be out of town?"

Daughter: "Mom! What am I going to do about the party?"

Do you get the sense that the members of this family are not all on the same page? As a result, they needlessly complicate their lives—which are already complicated enough—with crises of scheduling like this. How much simpler it would be if they kept a master calendar somewhere—yes, probably overseen by the mother—that brought together all the separate agendas of the family members: father's trip to headquarters, mother's work schedule, daughter's soccer schedule, and so on. Then when something like the party came along, it would be easy enough to check the calendar to see how such an event might be accommodated.

107

Better Check with Headquarters

If you're an executive, one helpful way to keep your family in the know is to bring your monthly calendar home from work. Also, your secretary could call your spouse and coordinate items on the calendar—especially ones that you're liable to forget. With the advent of computer networks, this type of communication should become even easier.

By the way, we have found that in almost every case in which a family has no calendar, it has no budget either. Thus the family has no guidelines for spending its time or its money. Is it any wonder, then, that such a family routinely finds itself in chaos and debt?

Go Over the Schedule Together Regularly

Keeping a calendar is pointless if you don't refer to it. The calendar is just a convenient way of recording the family's plans. But the record isn't what matters; *thinking* about the implications of family plans is what matters.

Some families find it helpful to review their plans for the upcoming week every Sunday evening. That way there is time to work out the details of the schedule and make adjustments if necessary. This need not be a long, drawn-out exercise. It may take as little as three or four minutes. But it's a way to avoid surprises.

Anticipate Annual Events

One of the worst burdens of frequent business travel is having to be away during important occasions in the life of the family, such as birthdays or anniversaries. Oftentimes, these absences are unavoidable. However, with a bit more planning, some travelers could easily minimize these scheduling conflicts. If they would look ahead and write down in their appointment books the important dates of the year, they could take those dates into consideration when planning their trips. They might be able to schedule the trips around the key events in their marriage and family life.

Even when absence cannot be avoided, it can at least be planned for. For instance, a husband learned that there was no way out of being gone for his anniversary, which was June 16. He would be tied up in a court case from the twelfth on, probably through the end of the month. So instead of making excuses and apologies to his wife, he arranged to spend the weekend before the twelfth with her at a resort hotel. It was not the same as being home on the sixteenth, but it was still a way to honor the occasion. (He also arranged for flowers and a card to be delivered on the sixteenth and made doubly sure to call home that evening!)

Or take another important date on the calendar: April 15. Everyone knows that is tax day. Yet how many travelers arrive home on the seventh or twelfth or even the fourteenth and suddenly wake up and say, "Gee, we need to do our taxes!" They then turn their home into an accounting fortress, browbeating their spouse to come up with receipts and other records and generally acting like the back end of Custer's mount to meet the deadline.

Wouldn't it be better to figure out in *January* exactly when those taxes are going to get done? Using travel as an excuse for not getting them done shows nothing but poor planning.

Become Experts at Contingency Planning

The suggestion to plan for contingencies may also seem self-evident to veteran travelers. The reality of travel is that nothing is certain except the unexpected. So as you and your family make plans, it's best to leave some room for "jiggle"—some flexibility in case things don't go exactly as you hoped.

Linda knew that her trade show at the Dallas Convention Center would wrap up by noon on February 3. She felt that would give her just enough time to jump in the car and make it home to Tulsa to host her daughter's birthday party. But she forgot to take into consideration one significant fact: Early February is prime season for severe ice storms in north Texas and Oklahoma. Consequently, when the weather deteriorated and the authorities closed the roads, her only recourse was to call home and console her very disappointed daughter.

Meanwhile, even as she was making that call, another birthday party was going on across town. Ironically, the mother in that family had been at the same convention as Linda and had been turned back by the same weather. But that woman had wisely recruited her sister and a neighbor to help her with the party. Consequently, even though she was prevented from traveling north, they were able to carry on without her. For the birthday girl, it was not the same without her mommy there—but at least her mommy was okay and had seen to it that the party would take place one way or another. That's contingency planning!

Don't Make Promises You Can't Keep

None of us likes to disappoint those we love. We like to accommodate their needs as best we can. But that sentiment brings us smack up against one of the hard realities of business travel: Trips don't always turn out the way we'd like them to. Planes and trains get delayed; sometimes they get cancelled. People change their minds about when a meeting is going to take place. Negotiations take longer than expected. Juries retire without rendering their verdicts. A major client shows up hours or even days late. A committee holds off on making a decision. A new opportunity suddenly opens up, demanding immediate action—and more time on the road.

When circumstances like these force a traveler to alter his or her plans in ways that affect the family, it can mean only one thing: Disappointments are inevitable. They can't be avoided. However, they can be minimized, or at least mitigated to some degree. A lot depends on what expectations the traveler has managed to create.

In our opinion, it's a mistake to tell your spouse or family that they can count on your presence at home if, in fact, there is a genuine possibility that you may not be able to be there. Which of these two conversations would you rather have?

Conversation 1

"But Dad, you *promised* you would be there! I told all the kids you would drive!"

"I know, Son, but I don't have much choice. This meeting is held over for a couple of days. Tell everyone I'm sorry."

Conversation 2

"But Dad, I was *hoping* you would be there! I told all the kids that if you were, you would drive!"

"I know, Son. I was hoping to be there, too. But I'm afraid this meeting is taking longer than I expected—just like I feared it would. Tell everyone I'm disappointed."

Frankly, we'd prefer never to have to go through either of these conversations. But if the choice is between being sorry and being disappointed, we'd opt for being disappointed. Being sorry means you committed but cannot follow through. Being disappointed means you *hoped* to be involved but made no guarantees. In our experience, family members can accept a few broken dreams—but not broken promises.

Attitude Adjustment

Bill's mom, Jeanne Hendricks, recognized that dealing with crushed hopes is a matter of both attitude and expectations. On the attitude side, she worked to develop in the Hendricks home an atmosphere in which family members recognized Dad's job as important. This helped to cultivate an attitude of appreciation. Jeanne explained to her four children that his job, which included heavy travel, was one way in which he expressed his commitment to the family. It enabled him to earn a living and support the family. While Jeanne's approach could not always remove disappointment when he had to be away, it at least made his absence easier to accept, because the kids knew their father was gone for reasons that benefited them.

9

Dollars and Nonsense

Finances

*I*n his book *His Needs, Her Needs,* Willard Harley pinpoints five basic needs men expect their wives to fulfill, and five needs wives expect their husbands to meet. The top five needs of women are instructive for our study of how business travel affects marriage, because right after a wife's needs for affection, conversation (communication), and honesty (trust and commitment) is her need for *financial support.*

Harley observes, "Humorous anecdotes abound on women who marry men for their money, but my counseling experience has taught me not to treat this tendency as a joke. In truth a woman *does* marry a man for his money—at least she wants him to earn enough money to support her as well as (or better than) her father did when she was growing up" (p. 116).

It is this very desire that keeps many a husband on the road today. Men who are salesmen, seminar speakers, performers, restaurant chain executives, and other road warriors often say that one of their primary motivations is the keen awareness that they have a wife and family to support back home.

Frankly, a similar impulse is driving more and more wives to travel on business, as well. The urge for stability in their family's finances outweighs the desire to stay home, strong as that desire might be. These women are committed to their jobs by virtue of the added income it brings, and if travel is part of the package, so be it!

However, while business travel is often a key part of earning a living, it also tends to create financial headaches of its own. Let's look at what happened to one couple who were earning good money but experienced financial discord nonetheless.

Double the Trouble

Jonathan and Rebecca would seem to have it made, financially speaking. He is working his way up the ladder in a prestigious management consulting firm. She is a reporter for a major urban newspaper. Their combined salaries place them among the top 15 percent of households in the country in terms of income, and as they have not yet started a family, they have plenty of money to spend as they please.

And they spend it! They've got the townhouse, the cars, the furniture, the clothes, the home entertainment center, the membership at the exclusive health club. When they are home, they like to dine on fresh pasta from a nearby gourmet takeout, accompanied by a nice bottle of Bordeaux. They vacation in Hawaii—or Nantucket, if they can get a beach house.

To a large extent, Jonathan and Rebecca look upon these purchases as well-deserved rewards for all their hard work. And they do work hard—which is to say, they travel hard. Rebecca logs countless miles covering her stories. Most of her travels are conducted at breakneck speed, forever racing to meet a deadline. Somehow, she always does, which is one reason why her editors like to put her on breaking news. They know she can be counted on to drop everything and get to the center of the action while events are still unfolding.

Jonathan's pace is slightly less hectic. His trips tend to require longer stays in one place—anywhere from two or three days to two weeks or more—as he visits clients to size up their needs and implement solutions. But when he is "on the ground" at a client's office, he is all business. Twelve- and fourteen-hour days are routine for him. "Gotta make the most of the time while you're there" is the way he figures it.

Needless to say, it takes a lot of effort and coordination for Jonathan and Rebecca to stay in touch. They are both very independent, so they seem to be able to get by even if they cannot (or do not) call each other every day. When they do connect, they spend much of their time bringing each other up to speed on their various pursuits.

However, one thing they rarely discuss—whether apart or home together—is finances. They have never said as much out loud, but in the back of their minds is the idea, "We're making plenty of money—enough that it's one of the least of our concerns."

Unfortunately, they should be making it one of their primary concerns. For the fact is, their finances are not in good shape. It is true they are making good money. But they also have a hefty mortgage to pay off on their townhouse, plus two car payments. Yet rather than pay down that debt and put money away in savings, they consume all their disposable income—and then some.

Some of this spending they justify, as we have seen, by virtue of their workload. But travel affects their spending in another way, too. On the road, they both find it easy and convenient to charge to their credit cards what seem to them to be small purchases—a bite to eat here, a couple of magazines there, a side trip to visit some popular local attraction. Obviously, their employers provide them with expense accounts. But those are fairly restrictive, paying only for business-related expenses. Thus, at the end of a trip it is not unusual for Jonathan or Rebecca to have spent thirty or forty dollars or more of their own money.

And because they rarely discuss finances (they don't have a budget), their combined credit card purchases mount up to significant sums each month. Neither one pays much attention to what the other is spending; indeed, neither one pays much attention to what he or she is spending. As a result, the credit card balances are slowly growing.

114

"Can You Make a Bigger Down Payment?"

The wake-up call comes when Rebecca decides to buy a new car. She picks out a popular (and expensive) four-wheel-drive vehicle and fills out a credit application.

But the next day, a loan representative is on the phone with some disturbing news: "I'm sorry, ma'am, but the underwriters will not accept your application. You'll have to put down about three times as much before they'll look at it."

"What!" Rebecca cries, shocked to the core. "What do you mean, they won't accept it?"

"Well, you're showing too much debt," says the loan officer.

Rebecca pauses, incredulous. "There must be some mistake! I know we've got a big house payment and all. But we've also got two incomes in this family. I mean, we've never not paid our bills, and—"

"I understand," says the loan officer, cutting her off. "But your consumer credit rating is what's killing you."

"What do you mean?" asks Rebecca.

"Well, in the first place, you've got an outstanding balance of nearly eighteen thousand dollars on one card and thirty-eight hundred on another. That might not be so bad, but twice within the last year they show you missed a couple of payments."

"We were *late* in paying them!" Rebecca is quick to stress. "We both travel a lot, and sometimes . . . well, sometimes it's true we don't get the check in the mail until we get back into town. But we're only talking maybe one or two days late, okay?"

"Well, that could be, but late payment is a no-no as far as the credit card companies are concerned—especially when the balance is so high."

"This is unbelievable!" intones Rebecca. "You're saying there's no way your company will give me a car loan?"

"Well, of course we'll give you a loan—as long as you can make a bigger down payment. Can you do that?"

Rebecca pauses to weigh her response. She knows she and Jonathan do not have near enough cash to make a down payment three times what she had planned. She had barely managed to scrape enough together to come up with the original amount.

Finally, she says, "I'll have to discuss this with my husband. He won't be back in town until tomorrow. I'll call you."

As Rebecca hangs up, waves of conflicting emotions begin washing over her. But the paramount feeling is anxiety. Eighteen thousand dollars on one card, thirty-eight hundred on the other! How in the world did that come about?

The next day, when Jonathan arrives home, he finds a note from Rebecca on the dining room table: "Welcome back, baby! Had to jump on that plane crash down south—should be back tomorrow. Hope so, anyway. Listen, we need to *talk* when I get in! They wouldn't make the loan for my car! Say we're too much in debt. Where's all our money going? I love you, Rebecca. P.S. Don't use the credit cards!"

The Number One Issue

Finances may be at the bottom of Jonathan and Rebecca's priorities (though that is probably about to change), but for most married couples, money is at the top of the list. At least, it causes the most trouble. A recent poll by Roper Starch Worldwide found that in the United States, money is the most common source of conflict between spouses. And research in the *Center for Marital and Family Studies Report* shows that coming into their marriages, new couples find money to be more of a problem than in-laws, jealousy, or communication. Four years later, they still find money to be the most troublesome aspect of marriage, ahead of communication, sex, and in-laws (in that order).

Thus, money dominates our thinking. This is true whether we have a lot of money or just a little (our status always being relative, of course, based on our perception). In fact, how a family discusses and deals with money-related matters is probably the most telling indication of how healthy that family is.

Here is a set of questions to stimulate your thinking in this regard.

1. How was money handled as you were growing up?
2. Who earned the money, and who was in charge of the budget?
3. How much money came in?

4. How were decisions made on how to spend the money?
5. What was usually done with the money (for example, saving, buying, squandering, donating, and so on)?
6. What values determined how money would be spent?
7. Were money problems discussed openly?
8. How were money problems handled?
9. What was the attitude toward debt, borrowing, credit cards, and saving?
10. Was money invested? If so, how?
11. Was insurance purchased? On whom or what? How much?
12. How were major purchases decided on? Who handled them?

We offer these questions for two reasons. First, the answers themselves are important. All of us, as couples, bring into our marriages the attitudes and values we picked up from our families while growing up. We also tend to follow the patterns and habits modeled for us by our parents. So by reflecting on the place of money in our background, we can gain some clues for tackling the troubles we may be having with money today.

Second, the *manner* in which we answer these questions tells a lot about our perspective on money. For example: Do we, as a couple, *discuss* issues like these? Have we *ever* discussed them? If so, what feelings tend to get stirred up by talk of money matters? Is there anxiety and tension? Are there fights and conflicts? Is there blame or denial? Or is there free and open communication, and feelings of confidence, trust, and mutual commitment to financial stability? If we've never discussed these issues, why not? Is there something we are avoiding?

Incidentally, avoidance isn't the only reason why couples tend to shy away from discussing certain aspects of their finances. We hear a lot today about how materialistic modern Americans have become, and it's hard to disagree with that assessment. Nevertheless, contrary to popular thinking, most people are not primarily motivated by money. Money plays an important role in their lives, to be sure. But money is not the main thing driving them. They are looking for other payoffs in life. Furthermore, they have other interests.

Jonathan and Rebecca are a case in point. Seen from one angle, they might be judged as just a couple of self-indulgent yuppies. Yet while it's true that they are spending more than they are making, their principal focus is not on making money or even on spending it. Truth be told, Jonathan lives to solve problems. That's what he's all about. Thus, his management consulting job is tailor-made for him. Meanwhile, Rebecca's preoccupation is with seeking adventure. She loves to travel and interview the prime players in a news story. It's the thrill of the hunt! That's what she seeks in life.

These insights help to explain why this couple is getting into financial trouble. It is not because they pay too much attention to money; *it is because they pay too little!* And while they may be an extreme example, they are far from alone. Even many couples who stick to a budget, live frugally, and pay all their bills on time often procrastinate when it comes to dealing with basic financial matters. Why? Because they are not motivated by financial matters! For them, reviewing the budget, evaluating household cash flow, planning for retirement, and the like rank right up there with mowing the lawn, cleaning out the gutters, and flossing their teeth.

The Hidden Costs of Business Travel

This being the case, business travel offers couples lots of reasons for not attending to their financial affairs. For one thing, many travelers getting ready to head out of town tend to "put on their game face" even before the day of departure. They start thinking about what they will encounter on the road, and soon they've already departed mentally and emotionally.

So when questions arise about bills to pay, checks to write, accounts to reconcile, and other details of financial management, these travelers can't be bothered. "I'll do it when I get back!" they say. But will they? Or will they then use their need to unwind from their trip as an excuse to put off responsibility even longer?

Travel has an insidious way of taking priority over everything else—even over things that ordinarily would come first. For example, one traveler knew in May that his car needed a brake job. But he kept putting off a trip to the shop, rationalizing (as so many

118

travelers do), "I can't waste time right now with repairs. I've got a trip coming up."

May slipped into June, and June into the dog days of summer. The business trips kept coming, and then a family vacation. It was early fall when his brakes were grinding so badly that he was forced to request a half day of personal time to take his car to the shop. Naturally, by that time the entire brake system needed to be rebuilt. Thus, a job that could have been done for under seventy-five dollars in May ended up costing several hundred dollars in September. All because of procrastination. Actually, allowing travel to determine his priorities was the mistake that really cost this man in terms of dollars, time, and aggravation.

We have seen how disruptive travel can be to communication in marriage. Yet managing the family finances depends on good communication between spouses and among family members. So it's not surprising that of all the problems that can result when partners fail to stay in touch, financial problems often top the list.

Here is a wife sitting at the kitchen table late at night, trying to figure out how she is going to pay a stack of bills that are due— and some that are past due. She's experiencing that classic sense of perplexity and anxiety that many of us feel when we come to the end of our paycheck before we come to the end of our month! She has a number of things she would like to discuss with her husband, but she hasn't heard from him in three days. He's the sort of traveler who thinks there's no need to call during a four-day trip. As he puts it, "It's not like the world is going to fall apart if she doesn't hear from me." That may be true. But if this couple's communication doesn't improve, their marriage may well fall apart.

Perceptions

One other way that business travel can affect a family's finances has to do with perceptions about how much things cost. The amenities of business travel vary widely, but generally speaking, the hospitality industry likes to convey to the traveler the sense that every effort has been made to pamper him or her, to meet every possible need—usually *in style.* Just take a look at some of the advertising directed toward travelers. You wouldn't want to show your family some of these ads, lest they think you really are going on vacation!

The impact of these accommodations on a traveler's thinking should not be underestimated. When you are catered to on the road, particularly at someone else's expense, it can be hard to suddenly switch gears when you return home, where the surroundings may not be so plush and where every expense comes out of your pocket. Thus many a traveler, upon returning from out of town, has succumbed to the temptation to extend the indulgences of the trip just a bit longer. The subtle mentality is, "I've enjoyed certain luxuries on the road; why shouldn't I enjoy them at home?"

We saw hints of this pattern in Jonathan and Rebecca's situation. They felt a sense of entitlement about their spending. They saw their purchases as a reward for hard work. Indeed, many travelers take the attitude, "I *owe* it to myself to buy this item . . . pay for this service . . . enjoy this amenity. After all, I've earned it!" But there's a danger in that way of thinking. Certainly, there's a time and place for kicking back and relaxing after a long, grueling trip. But the idea that we work in order to justify rewards is a rather empty way to live. It suggests that our work has no other purpose than to afford us self-indulgent treats.

However, not all travelers lavish their free-spending ways on themselves. As we noted earlier, the number one emotion experienced by frequent flyers is guilt. One can imagine that for many travelers, this feeling stems from a perception that by being on the road—and *enjoying* it, no less!—they are somehow failing their spouse and family back home. To assuage this guilt, many of these travelers purchase gifts to take home that they really cannot afford, to "make up" for being gone. There's nothing wrong with gifts; we think bringing something home for each member of the family is a good idea. But there's definitely something wrong when guilt is the motive behind these purchases. And when the cost of the items ends up breaking the household budget, how does that contribute to the family's well-being?

120

Keeping Your Feet on the Ground

By now, you should have some feel for how business travel may be affecting your personal finances. Your troubles may be as "minor" as keeping the bills paid on time or as major as skyrocketing credit card debt. Whatever the case, here are a few tips from frequent flyers who, even at thirty thousand feet, have learned what it takes to keep their feet on the ground financially.

Establish a Budget

Developing a budget and keeping a schedule (suggested in chapter 8) are probably two of the most obvious ideas in this book. That does not mean they are commonly practiced!

So if you already have a budget and a schedule—fantastic! We applaud you with great fanfare! You are doing two of the simplest and most basic things anyone could do to prevent travel from harming their marriage.

If you don't have a budget and a schedule, *why not?* You see, it would be easy for someone, upon reading this suggestion, to throw this book aside with the attitude, "A budget?! That's their first tip? Wow, talk about stating the obvious! I thought this book would really give me some *new* ideas for dealing with the stress that business travel places on my marriage."

But what good are new ideas if well-worn, tried-and-true ideas are not being implemented? Establishing a budget is about as fundamental as it gets when it comes to gaining control over personal finances. It is *the* place to start. No serious businessperson would try to run a business without keeping track of the finances—the revenue, the expenses, the cash flow, the accounts payable, and so on. Yet it's amazing how many astute businesspeople allow their personal finances to become an absolute mess!

We won't take time to go through the steps of how to develop a budget. There are plenty of other resources available to assist you in that effort. But we implore any reader whose family does not have a budget—or has one but doesn't follow it—to put that crucial piece of planning in place and stick to it! Any other advice concerning finances will be of little value apart from that basic practice.

On the next page is a simple worksheet to get you started on a budget.

Category	Monthly Budget	Annual Budget	Percentage of Total Budget
Income			
Gross Income			
Interest Income			
Miscellaneous Income			
Total Income			
Expenses			
Charitable Contributions			
Clothing			
Credit & Loans			
Credit Card			
Credit Card			
Car Loan			
Miscellaneous Credit			
Miscellaneous Credit			
Food & Toiletries			
Health & Medical			
Household Items & Repair			
Insurance			
Auto			
Life			
Other			
Miscellaneous			
Mortgage Payment (or Rent)			
Personal Expenses			
You			
Your Spouse			
Child			
Child			
Child			
Postage & Delivery			
Recreation & Eating Out			
Subscriptions			
Taxes			
Federal			
State			
Local			
Telephone			
Transportation, Parking, & Auto			
Utilities			
Gas			
Electric			
Water			
Other			
Other			
Vacation			
Total Expenses			
Income Less Expenses			
Savings			

Fill Out Expense Reports Immediately

In our experience, expense reports are the bane of most travelers' existence. Indeed, one traveler's vision of hell is to spend eternity filling out endless expense reports for his company's accounting department—the cruelest torture of all being that he must submit original receipts, which, of course, the poor soul has lost!

Our purpose is not to try to put a happy face on what is, admittedly, a less than pleasant task for most of us. Expense accounting is a doleful bit of housekeeping that just has to be done. But one reason for doing it is to prevent needless personal expenses.

For most business travelers, expenses on the road divide into two categories: those the employer will pay for (such as transportation, lodging, a per diem for meals) and those the traveler must pay for (such as newspapers and magazines, shoe shines, liquor). To an outsider, these would seem to be easily distinguished and accounted for. But after several days on the road, with receipts floating around in your wallet, pants pockets, suit pockets, briefcase, date book, suitcase, and who knows where else, and having made some cash outlays with no receipt (such as tips, phone calls, a box of popcorn between flights at O'Hare)—it can be a nightmare to come up with a final reckoning!

Every traveler will have to come up with his or her own system for keeping track of these expenses. But it's important to have one. We believe it is both a moral and personal responsibility to accurately account for each business expense. It stands to reason that the sooner you prepare this formal accounting, the easier it will be to remember what an expense was for and who was to pay for it. Conversely, after two or three weeks, when your mind is focused on other matters and when maybe another trip or two has come and gone, it can be impossible to recall exactly what was spent. Quite often, the traveler is the loser—which means his or her family loses because the family's finances are affected.

In this regard, many companies have time limits for submitting reimbursement requests. So procrastinators are playing a risky game. Yet we've known people to boast that they would rather give up ten or twenty dollars in reimbursements than fill out the necessary forms. Obviously, amounts like that probably will not bust a family budget. But the practice does convey a certain attitude about money and fiscal responsibility.

Schedule Check Writing and Bill Payment

Sometime during their early days of marriage, most couples tend to divide household chores between them, including check writing and bill payment. (If you and your spouse have not decided on who should be responsible for that duty, we suggest one of you accept the task, as it will simplify things enormously.)

Because travel throws a lot of complications into a family's life, we suggest you *schedule* exactly when you plan to pay your bills each month. That way, you can plan in terms of your cash flow, and around the disruptions of travel. This is especially important if the one who keeps the books is the person who travels, or travels the most. Remember Rebecca's excuses about making a couple of late payments? Those delinquencies occurred not because Rebecca was an inherently irresponsible person but because she neglected to coordinate household management with her busy travel schedule.

Review Your Finances before the Traveler Leaves

We encourage you to go over your finances and anticipate your needs as best you can when you know a trip is coming. Look ahead to the financial events in the near future: bills to be paid, amounts to be received, forms or reports to be filed (such as taxes). Ask yourself, How will these matters be affected by this trip? Who will pay the bills? When? Will there be money in the checking account to pay them? Will a check need the traveler's signature? If so, how will that be arranged?

Not every trip affords a couple time to stop and think this way. Some occupations require people to drop everything on a moment's notice and head out of town. If you or your spouse have a job like that, it becomes especially important for you as a couple to establish a plan for taking care of financial responsibilities in the traveler's absence. In most cases, it would probably work best for the spouse at home to handle the family finances. But even then, he or she needs to know the expectations and preferences of the traveler regarding the management of affairs at home.

Prepare a Crisis Plan

If, God forbid, something should happen to the traveler, what measures are in place to allow the family to carry on without him or her?

In our opinion, travelers owe their families some sense of security. This involves more than financial security, though it certainly includes that. We're talking about preparations for the unexpected, a crisis plan that hopefully will never have to be used but thankfully will be there if it is needed.

A whole chapter could be devoted to the development of this plan. But a few of the basic elements include:

- information on where important documents are kept—items such as a will, a mortgage, insurance papers, tax documents, instructions concerning life support, and so on;
- a list of key professionals in the family's life and their phone numbers—people such as the traveler's physician, attorney, accountant, insurance agent, and so on;
- a summary of the family's finances, including bank accounts, credit accounts, stocks, and other investments;
- instructions concerning the traveler's wishes for burial, in the event of his or her death.

Evaluate All the Costs of Travel

There's no getting around the fact that certain jobs require travel. Consequently, many people who work in those jobs just accept the rigors of the road as part of the deal.

Certainly anyone who must travel to earn a living ought to be reasonably comfortable with being on the road, away from his or her spouse and family. Yet having said that, there are often hidden costs connected with travel that are not always considered, either by travelers or their employers.

Among these hidden costs is the emotional wear and tear that being on the road places on a traveler—and on his or her family.

This book looks at a dozen areas in which travel causes stress in marriage and family relationships. Unfortunately, the emotional cost is too often overlooked when it comes to evaluating the worth of a job. For example, a traveler may only look at the income and benefits of the position, ignoring the fact that time away from home may cost him or her a marriage.

More pernicious is the tendency among some people in the corporate world to use travel as a badge of commitment. We know of executives who actually compete to rack up the most frequent flyer miles, the premise being that time on the road somehow displays more fortitude and fitness for senior leadership than time at the home base. Even families get evaluated in this regard: Promotions may be contingent on whether an employee's spouse and children have shown themselves to be "tough enough" to endure the absence of the employee due to travel.

There is much we could say to employers in this regard. But if you are a traveler, we encourage you to periodically evaluate your job and conduct a cost-to-benefits analysis to see whether the job is as rewarding as it needs to be. Said another way: Is your current position, with its requirement for travel, satisfactory to you *and* your family? Or is it demanding more of you and of them than you, as a family, are willing to give?

These are hard questions, and we realize they have the potential to stir up trouble. But this book is, after all, an appeal to take seriously the impact of business travel on marriage and family life. Sometimes that impact is severe. When it is, everyone loses—traveler, spouse, family, employer. Wouldn't it be better to face facts and, if necessary, find some other occupation or position that does not require travel—or as much travel—to support your family and create value for your employer, rather than sacrifice loved ones on the altar of financial gain?

10

Keep the Home Fires Burning!

Sexual Intimacy and Romance

*H*umorist Dave Barry says that whenever he hears about a couple who have, say, nine children, he never wonders, "How do they manage to take care of them all?" Instead he asks, "Where did they find time to *conceive* them all?" (If you have even one child, you know what that can mean for your sex life!)

A similar situation applies to business travel. If you ever hear a frequent traveler or his or her spouse claiming to have a great sex life, you can pretty much figure that (a) it's a lie, or (b) they've figured out some things from which we can all benefit!

Business travel contributes to a married couple's romantic intimacy about as much as does a teenager in the next room or a toddler down the hall. It proves highly disruptive, and if a couple does not take steps to safeguard their sex life, they can find themselves drifting apart—with all the dangers that entails.

Consider the case of Marcus and Ellen. Their marriage is basically sound, which is a good thing since Marcus's travel schedule places a lot of stress on it. One of the hardest challenges they face is that the timing of their intimacy is thrown off. Let's see how.

"Honey, I'm Home!"

Marcus is a frustrated lover. He and his wife, Ellen, haven't had sex in more than a month, and he's not happy about it. Worst of all, his best efforts at initiating intimacy seem to have blown up in his face. He doesn't understand what's happened.

Part of the problem, as Marcus well knows, is that he has been out of town for most of the month. He works for a firm of consulting engineers. As a junior-level member specializing in highway projects, Marcus spends most of his time at work sites, advising contractors and overseeing the quality of their work. His schedule for the month has been: two weeks at a job in Dallas, two days at home, three days in Missouri, five days in Atlanta, one day at home, two days back in Dallas, and two days at a satellite office in Toronto.

Needless to say, this pace has wreaked havoc on Marcus and Ellen's sex life. Out of twenty-nine days, they have spent only three together.

Marcus's first stopover fell on a weekend. He had come home from the airport hoping (actually, assuming) that he and Ellen would soon be making mad, passionate love. Indeed, he had had sex on his mind all during the ride home in the airport shuttle. After paying the driver, he had come through the front door with his customary "Honey, I'm home!" shouting it out with a certain suggestiveness in his voice, as if to say, "You lucky thing!"

But Ellen had not been home. Their daughter, Tracy, had run into a swarm of yellow jackets, and Ellen had taken her to the emergency room. Fortunately, the girl was not seriously harmed. But the experience had completely frazzled Ellen's nerves, and she was in no mood for sex that day.

The following day, Sunday, Marcus and Ellen decided to sleep in. When they finally began to stir, Marcus rolled over and began caressing his wife affectionately, hoping that it would lead to intercourse. And for a while, they did enjoy a tender moment. But just as Ellen was beginning to get as aroused as Marcus was, the sound of little feet came thumping down the hall, and the bedroom door burst open.

"Daddy's home!" Tracy shouted as she leaped into her parents' bed.

The moment for passion was lost. Nor would it return. As Ellen was finishing her coffee after breakfast, she asked Marcus when he would be leaving for the airport.

"Oh, about four o'clock," he mumbled from behind his Sunday paper.

"Uh-huh," Ellen replied. "Well, I was thinking. How about if we had a picnic over at the river walk today? It's nice weather."

Upon hearing the word *picnic,* little Tracy perked up her ears. "A picnic?" she shouted. "Oh, boy! Can we, Daddy? Can we?" She was jumping up and down.

"Huh? What?" Marcus came out from behind his paper. "What did you say?"

"I wanted to know whether you'd like to go on a picnic," Ellen repeated.

"Yeah, uh, I guess so." Marcus shrugged his shoulders and made a face, as if he didn't care one way or the other. Then he suddenly frowned. "Wait a minute! My game's on at noon. You know, my brother's coming over, and we were planning to watch—"

He broke off as soon as he saw the crestfallen look come over Ellen's face. But it was too late. He watched her jaw set in anger.

"You're barely home two days, and you want to spend one of those with your brother, watching a stupid football game?"

"It's not *all day!*" Marcus began protesting. "We're talking a couple of hours!" He began racking his brain for a way out of this mess. "Look, I'll go on a picnic if you want to. Let's just, uh, do it a little earlier."

"It's already almost ten o'clock, Marcus! And we just finished breakfast!"

"So we'll eat a light lunch."

"Or you could skip the first part of the game!"

"But it's a game that may decide the playoffs!" he replied defensively. "Besides, my brother said he'd be here at noon."

"Fine! I hope you guys enjoy the game!"

In the end, the couple managed to patch things up. Marcus compromised and agreed to miss the first quarter of the game to take a walk with his family. But later, as his plane was taking off, he realized that somehow he had come home and left town again without making love to his wife.

His second stopover had only been overnight. That time, *he* had been the reluctant partner. Something he had eaten disagreed with him, and after arriving home, he had gone right to bed, feeling nauseous.

Timing Is Everything

Now Marcus is back from Toronto, and it appears he will be home for ten full days. This time he has set aside the first evening, Thursday night, to spend with Ellen. Dinner and a movie. "That should put her in the mood," he thinks.

But the evening doesn't work out that way. First, there's an unusually long wait for a table at the restaurant. And when they finally sit down, the service is slow. Waiting for their dinners, they begin to feel anxious about finishing in time to get to the theater.

As a result, throughout the meal their conversation remains terse and superficial. Ellen makes small talk about Tracy, the neighbors, her sister, whatever. Marcus mumbles one-word responses as he wolfs down his food. After paying the check, they rush to the theater, just in time for the start of the picture.

Three-fourths of the way through the movie, Ellen leans over and whispers, "How much longer is this going to be?"

Marcus looks at his watch. "I don't know. Another fifteen minutes, maybe."

"I told the sitter we'd be home by nine-thirty. She has to be home by ten."

Marcus doesn't respond. But it is almost 9:45 when the final credits begin to roll. The couple race home.

When Marcus returns from taking the sitter home, he expects to make love with Ellen before going to bed. But to his surprise—and disappointment—she resists his advances. "Let's just talk for a while," she says.

130

"Talk? I'm too tired to talk! Besides, I've got to get up and go to the office tomorrow."

Ellen doesn't say anything.

"What—are you angry at me?" Marcus asks.

"No, I'm not angry! I just want to talk for a little bit. We haven't talked all evening!"

Marcus rolls his eyes. "What do you mean? What about dinner?" He shakes his head in frustration. "I don't understand, Ellen. I take you out for dinner and a show. I spend the evening with you—the first time we've been out in a month. Now I come home and want a little romance, and you just want to talk!"

"I didn't say that. I just think I'd enjoy it more if we could ease into it by talking a little bit first."

"Well, if the choice is between talking about it or doing it, I'd rather do it!"

Ellen remains quiet, staring at the bed. Finally, Marcus heads for the bathroom, mumbling to himself, "I can see nothing's going to happen tonight!"

The next day, Marcus is up early and off to the office. That night, he and Ellen have a church social to attend. By the time they get home, they are both so exhausted that they fall into bed and go right to sleep.

Then comes Saturday. As Marcus wipes his mouth after breakfast, he turns to Ellen and asks, "Do you remember that promise I made last month?"

"You mean the one about working on things I need you to do?"

"Exactly! I believe you call it your 'honey do' list."

Ellen's face bursts into a smile. "I haven't forgotten!"

"Well, believe it or not, neither have I. Did you happen to make a list for this weekend?" he asks, hoping against hope that she hasn't.

Hardly able to contain herself, Ellen goes over to the kitchen counter. "Actually, I did make a list," she says as she hunts in a drawer. A moment later, she produces a notepad with a dozen or so items written on it. Placing it on the table in front of Marcus, she hugs him warmly and plants a big kiss on his cheek. "Thank you for remembering!"

Marcus spends the rest of the morning working through the projects on the list. He replaces the porch light. He cleans out the bathroom drain. He clears the cobwebs from the upper corners in the garage. He troubleshoots the quirky garage door opener. By lunchtime he has crossed about two-thirds of the items off the list.

"Do you really need me to take the dog in for a shampoo *today?*" he asks as she serves him a huge bowl of homemade soup. "You know I hate to go in there. The women that run that place just talk my ear off!"

"That's why I want you to go. I don't have time."

"Like I do?"

"I know it's a sacrifice, honey. But Snuffles really needs a wash, and I figure you'll do a better job of getting out of there than I will. Besides," she adds with a smile and a gentle pat on his wrist, "those ladies think you're so cute. It'll make their day!"

"I can see you're not jealous!"

"Why should I be? I've got you all to myself!" She cocks her head to the side with a mock pout. "Please? For *me*, would you do it?"

"*Only* because it's for you!"

That evening, it is late when Ellen, Marcus, and Tracy finally sit down for dinner. Marcus is bushed and eats at a slow, relaxed pace. He and Ellen sit and talk long after they finish, while Tracy sits on her mother's lap. Eventually, Tracy nods off, and Ellen takes her up to her room to put her to bed.

Marcus begins clearing dishes and loading the dishwasher. As he is wiping down the counter, he hears Ellen clear her throat. Turning, he finds her standing in the kitchen doorway, wearing a shimmering black negligee.

"Hi," she says softly, with a gentle smile. "I want you!" Then she turns to go upstairs.

The next morning, Marcus watches his wife as she sips her coffee. "Can I ask you something? Why were you so disinterested in making love on Thursday, after we went out, but not last night? I mean, we just stayed home last night. There was nothing special going on or anything."

"I didn't feel like it on Thursday," Ellen replies. "It was just too . . . too much rushing, too much tension. I just wasn't ready."

"Well, I sure was!" Marcus sighs, mindful of the monthlong frustration he had endured.

"Last night was different. I felt . . . well, I felt like I wanted to be with you. I mean, we talked after dinner. You did all those things on my 'honey do' list."

"*Most* of them!" Marcus gently corrects, not wanting to leave anything open for questioning.

"All right, *most* of them. You took Snuffles in for a shampoo."

Marcus laughs. "*That* put you in the mood for sex? In that case, I'll make sure you have the cleanest dog in town!"

"That's not what I mean, and you know it! I just like it when you pay attention to me. You're gone so much. When you come home, it's like we have to get reacquainted all over again. I'm usually not ready to just hop into bed."

"Yeah, well, I guess that's the difference between me and you."

"It is. You're right. We're very different in that way." Then Ellen adds, "And if you want me to make love to you, you'll have to pay attention to that."

Somehow her remark did not sound like a threat. It sounded more like a plea. A plea to get what she—and he—really wanted.

To Know and Be Known

In discussing sexual intimacy and romance, we are keenly aware that fools rush in where angels fear to tread. Other issues of marriage may be wide open for giving and taking directions, but it is dangerous to dispense advice when it comes to sex.

In the first place, there are so many "experts" on this topic that anything we might say has probably already been said. Moreover, anything we might suggest has probably been contradicted by someone somewhere—backed up, no doubt, by a statistic! So who can anyone trust for accurate information?

Still, we believe there are some fundamental truths about the sexual aspect of marriage that have proved themselves reliable and stood the test of time. Therefore, while we may be cautious about rushing into this issue, we will not shy away from it. It is too important for a healthy relationship.

People have been giving opinions on the nature and significance of sex for as long as . . . well, for as long as there has been sex to make new people! Sex has been written about, painted, sculpted, filmed, and studied. It has been praised and cursed, elevated and debased, idolized and trivialized. And oh yes, above all else—*tried!*

So what have humans learned from this in-depth study of the subject? In our view, two lessons stand out: *commitment* and *romance.* Without those, sex is ultimately meaningless. It's empty. Without the prospect of a committed, ongoing relationship, sex is just a pointless game played by bodies rather than people. Likewise, without emotional intimacy, sex is just a physical act—one that may not even be pleasurable.

The point is that sex has something to do with our very personhood as human beings. Sure, it involves hormones and bodily functions and the possibility of making babies. But there is something more going on than biology. The two bodies coming together seem to be a powerful means toward an even more powerful end. We believe that ultimate end is intimacy—the sense of oneness and completion that two people experience when they know and are known by one another.

Like Trying to Light a Candle in the Wind

Travel thoroughly disrupts intimacy. It may not destroy it, but it certainly interferes with it. It does so by affecting every aspect of the relationship that contributes to sexual intimacy.

For example, travel impedes communication. Think of the times when you and your spouse have been unable to talk because travel has taken you apart. Whatever it was you wanted to talk about—kids, money, in-laws, the schedule, a conflict, a cause for rejoicing, or maybe you *just wanted to talk*—how did being prevented from talking affect your attitude toward sex once you were reunited with your partner? In all likelihood, sex was no longer your most pressing need. Communication was. You needed communication before you could have a good sexual experience.

Or what about commitment and trust? Those are absolute requirements for sustaining a satisfying sexual relationship. It's impossible to give yourself unreservedly to someone you cannot trust. Yet along comes a business trip, and suddenly commitment is tested. There is the obvious temptation of infidelity. But there is also the distance that is suddenly introduced into the relationship. Not just the physical distance but the emotional distance that comes from living apart, from experiencing things that are not shared with your mate. No wonder, as Ellen put it, a couple has to get "reacquainted all over again" before they can fully enjoy each other.

And then there's the fact that travel disrupts our time. Marcus and Ellen certainly felt the impact of that. Perhaps you and your spouse do, too. As humans, we have a way of calculating worth by using a clock. The more time spent on something, the more important it must be. But what if that "something" happens to be us and our marriage? If there is little time devoted to the relationship, we can only conclude that it must not matter very much—that *we* do not matter very much. Travel robs us of time—and if we let it, it will rob us of intimacy. And there goes our sex life.

We are not saying that business travel makes it impossible to have a healthy sexual relationship with your spouse. But it does prevent you from freely and spontaneously engaging in sex when your relationship calls for it. (This is one of the worst aspects of business travel and also one of the least recognized. For example, it never dawns on those who perceive travel as glamorous that it interferes with your sex life. Contrary to popular opinion, travel is anything but sexy. It actually deters ideal sex!)

In the end, how you and partner react to the stress that travel places on your sex life probably says a lot about your relationship. If the relationship is healthy, the disruption that travel causes is liable to create *anticipation:* You can't wait to get back together and embrace each other in passion. If the marriage is unhealthy, travel may mean *temptation:* Free of your spouse, you may start looking around at other possibilities.

What if your marriage is in between—just sort of mediocre? In that case, perhaps the most common experience is *frustration and irritation:* Travel serves to remind you how much you need your partner, but the relationship is not very satisfying when you come together again. If that describes your situation, we suggest that you not fold your hands and do nothing. Take action! Sit down and talk with your partner. Go away together for a weekend to evaluate your lives and discuss how to get things jump-started. Read a book on marriage together. Make an appointment with a counselor. Do *something!* But don't ignore a lackluster relationship. If you do, you may wake up one day with no relationship at all.

Keeping the Home Fires Burning

There are a lot more factors than business travel that cause couples to lose interest in having sex. As someone has noted, sex evolves over the years from triweekly to try weekly—and ultimately to try weakly! At least, that's the experience of too many couples.

We're not going to suggest "a hundred and one ways to improve your sex life." But we offer three basic principles for keeping the home fires burning when business travel threatens to douse them.

1. Protect Your Sexual Intimacy

As a couple, make up your mind that you will protect your sexual intimacy. We are dead serious when we say there are countless factors that can cause you and your spouse to lose interest in having sex. Every couple must wage a war to defend what they have together. Their enemies include interruptions of all kinds, misunderstandings and communication breakdowns, memories from the past, fears about the future, financial problems (and successes), diseases and accidents, emotional turmoil, the intrusion of war and calamity. The list goes on and on.

Unless a couple decides up front that they are going to hold on to each other—both figuratively and literally—they are liable to let their intimacy slide, to the point where sex becomes little more than a chore, if it is not forgotten altogether.

This brings us to the matter of sexual temptation. As baby boomers, we grew up in a generation that adopted an extremely permissive attitude toward sex. That attitude is still around today. And while there is a cultural expectation for married couples to honor their marriage vows, there tends to be a casual, wink-wink, nod-nod posture toward "fooling around." People joke about it, write best-selling books about it, get on TV and boast about it.

Nevertheless, in our view there is no substitute for faithfulness. We've sat and talked with too many people whose lives have been shattered by adultery to feel otherwise. We've listened to too many

136

stories of heartache and pain, of spouses who have thrown away their lives on a worthless affair, of people who will have a hard time ever trusting again because they've been cheated on, of children whose lives have been permanently affected by the selfish choices of a wayward parent.

On the other hand, we feel privileged to know of many couples who have remained faithful over the years, sticking with each other through thick and thin, building intimacy and trust. Not that they have always led perfect lives. Sometimes they have had to learn the hard way, and forgiveness has been an important part of the process. But one thing these couples have in common is that they have made a commitment—and a recommitment—to faithfulness.

We would not for a minute deny or even minimize the reality of sexual temptation. It's out there, no doubt about it! Nor would we present ourselves as saints in this regard. We too face those temptations. But it's because we face them that we reaffirm the importance of protecting what we have at home.

In our experience, keeping the home fires burning takes commitment. It means both partners choose to hold on to each other and to the special intimacy they enjoy.

2. Concentrate on the Relationship

Concentrate on the relationship more than on the sex. This is a lesson that Ellen is helping Marcus learn. Marcus thinks that if he and Ellen just had sex more when he was home, everything else in their relationship would work out fine. But he's wrong! The only thing that would change would be the frequency of sex. Would that improve the relationship? Hardly.

But look what happens when Marcus takes time to treat Ellen as a person—when he listens to her, does things for her, and tells her about himself. Now there is closeness and intimacy. They are sharing life together. Their experience has meaning. Result? A vastly more satisfying relationship *and* better sex. Indeed, paying attention to the relationship *leads* to the better sex. That's almost always the way the equation works—not the other way around.

3. Pay Attention to Chronic Problems

Part of protecting sexual intimacy is dealing with recurring sexual problems. It's impossible to preserve intimacy if something keeps hammering on it relentlessly.

For example, throughout her married life, Judith has struggled with being frigid; she withdraws almost every time her husband, Nick, initiates sex. Occasionally she tolerates his lovemaking, but she does so reluctantly. She certainly does not enjoy the moment. In fact, she has never had an orgasm while having intercourse.

This situation does not bode well for the future of Nick and Judith's relationship, with or without travel. But it certainly compounds the problems that travel introduces into this couple's sex life. For one thing, it is causing Judith to stay on the road more than she needs to. She claims she is just trying to build her career, that she'll "settle down" eventually. But the truth is that travel is a way for her to avoid sexual intimacy with Nick.

Our strong advice to someone like Judith would be to seek out professional help from someone trained to deal with problems of a sexual nature. Other such problems would include impotency, premature ejaculation, inability to achieve orgasm, pain during intercourse, loss of sex drive—really, anything that impedes the normal, satisfying expression of sexual affection.

Sex was never intended to be a chore; it should certainly not be a burden. We believe sex was meant to be a celebration, both an expression of joy and a source of joy for a couple committed to sharing life together.

11

Look! Up in the Sky! It's a Bird! It's a Plane! It's My Parent!

Parenting

*I*n 1978, Boeing Aircraft commissioned a study to investigate the emotional dynamics of frequent business flyers. The research found that the leading psychological characteristic of these travelers was feelings of guilt.

It's not hard to imagine why. There are many possible explanations for that guilt. But high on the list would have to be the sense that, as travelers, we are neglecting or being unfair to our family by being on the road.

If you have small children, you know what it feels like to walk away from the family car at the airport, with the crying or even screaming of your little ones echoing in your ears. You wonder if you are not abandoning your spouse and leaving your kids in the lurch, orphaning them just when they need you most. And if you have teens, you know the sullen look they are liable to give you as you walk out the door. It's as if they were saying, "Yeah, there you go again. Off to conquer the world. Don't worry about me. I'll get by—without you!"

To be sure, not all travelers feel guilt, nor do all children feel anxious or resentful about their parent's having to be away. But there's no getting around the fact that the greatest toll for many who travel on business is the emotional strain that travel places on them as parents. We could offer countless stories in support of this fact. Here is one.

Where's Dad?

Casey has a dull headache, the kind that comes from not getting enough sleep the night before. Yet it was tough for her to get much sleep after her little boy, Jason, started throwing up after dinner the night before. The sickness ended within a couple of hours. But all night long, Casey found herself jumping up and rushing to his bedside every time she thought she heard him stirring.

Now she is feeling the effects of that ordeal as she keys documents in the law office where she works. Glancing at her watch for about the twentieth time today, she sees it is only 2:38 P.M. "Can I make it another two hours?" she wonders.

Not that her day will improve much once she leaves work. She will fight her way through traffic to pick up her son from day care, then fight her way home. But at least the cool, rainy air outside will be a relief, and she won't have to use her brain. "If I could just get some sleep!" she muses longingly.

Then her extension rings, and she takes the call. After listening for a moment, she exclaims, "Oh no! Please don't tell me that!" She listens a moment longer. "Can't he hold on for just a little while longer?" Finally she puts down the phone.

Shaking her head, she turns to her coworker at the next desk and says, "Can you believe it? I've got to go get Jason from day care. He's sick again!"

Suddenly Casey's wish to get away has turned to reluctance. And no wonder: She will have to approach her supervisor to explain her need to leave. This has happened twice before within the last six weeks. But fortunately for Casey, the supervisor herself has had to go to a doctor's appointment. So Casey manages to break away and heads into the snarled traffic.

140

At home, she puts Jason to bed and then makes herself a cup of tea. "Madeline should be home pretty soon," she thinks as she reflects on her daughter's schedule. Madeline is fifteen—going on eighteen! In Casey's mind, Madeline redefines the meaning of the word *independent*. "Just like her father," Casey often remarks.

Casey's husband, Jim, is a sales representative for a company that manufactures store fixtures and displays. He drives about thirty thousand miles a year, visiting retailers in the region. This week is typical: He left Monday morning and won't be back until late Thursday night. It's been that way for a dozen years.

Casey closes her eyes and begins to nod off. But not for long. She snaps to attention when Jason cries out. He has vomited once again. Casey helps him clean up and get back to bed.

By now, it is time to start preparing dinner. Not that Casey has much appetite. But Madeline will need to eat. In fact, she should have been home by now. Casey hunts through the refrigerator and pantry and finally starts fixing spaghetti.

Time rolls by. She flips on the evening news, paying particular attention to the weather. When the news is over, a game show starts. By now, Casey is starting to get hungry—and angry that Madeline is still not home. She fixes herself a plate of spaghetti and sits back down in front of the TV.

Finally, at 7:10, Madeline comes through the front door. "Hey, Mom!" she yells automatically as she starts heading for her room.

"And just where have you been?" Casey demands angrily, jumping up from the couch. "It's past seven o'clock!"

"Mom, chill!" Madeline replies patronizingly. "I was just over at Sheila's, okay?"

"No, it's not okay! Not when I don't know about it."

"But you know Sheila."

"Yes—I *know* Sheila! That's what I'm talking about."

"Look, if you want to get down on my friends—"

"I'm not down on your friends. But you don't go over to someone's house without letting me know."

"Mom, I'm not a little kid anymore!"

"Were Sheila's parents there?" Casey asks, ignoring the last comment.

"I don't know."

"Yes, you do know! Were they or weren't they?"

"Okay! No! They both had to work late."

"You know I don't like you over at someone's house by yourself."

"Mom, we weren't by ourse—I mean, I wasn't by *my*self. I mean, uh, Sheila was there."

"And who else?"

"Oh . . . Sheila's brother."

"And who else?"

"Nobody, really. Just a couple of kids from school."

"Who?"

"What is this, a police lineup?"

"Who else were you over there with?" Casey presses.

Madeline thinks through what to say. Then finally she blurts out, "Okay! There were a couple of boys from school over there, if you just *have* to know! Okay? Sheila and I were playing computer games with a couple of boys. What did you *think* we were doing?"

"Madeline, you know we've talked about this before. Your father and I have made a rule that you are not to be at anyone's house with boys without their parents home—and without calling us!"

"Yeah, you and your rules! I like the way you make up rules when Daddy's away. When he leaves town, it's like you turn into my watchdog or something!"

"I have no interest in being a watchdog! It's just that when Daddy's away, I have to see that you stay out of trouble."

Madeline rolls her eyes and turns away.

"Don't you walk away!" Casey warns her. "We're not done talking."

"What else is there to say?" Madeline asks, shrugging her shoulders.

Casey starts to reply, when she hears another cry from Jason's room. "We'll finish this discussion later," she says as she goes to help him. But Madeline knows the "discussion" is over, and she goes back to her room.

Later, when Jim calls home, Casey reviews her day and dwells at length on the incident with Madeline, repeating the conversation word for word. Sitting in his motel room, hundreds of miles away, Jim can hear the weariness and exasperation in his wife's voice. He feels especially uneasy when she says, "Honey, I'm worried about our daughter. I'm really afraid she's getting herself into trouble!"

"Yeah, I understand," he replies. "I'll talk with her when I get home."

"I don't know what you're going to say that will change her behavior," Casey shoots back. "She's not listening to me. Why should she listen to you?"

"'Cause I'm her father."

Casey pauses a moment. "I don't think that's how she feels."

"What do you mean?"

"I think she's unhappy that you're gone."

"Well, what am I supposed to do?"

"I'm not blaming you! I'm just telling you how I think Madeline feels about it."

After they say good-bye, Jim hangs up, turns off the lamp over the nightstand, and slips under the covers of his bed. He has a long drive in the morning and needs to get up early. But he has a hard time falling asleep. The tensions of his own day are weighing down on him. Now he has the added burden of Casey's anxiety about their daughter. He senses that his wife is feeling less and less adequate to the task of raising a teenage girl—to say nothing of little Jason.

"And here you are, off on another trip!" a voice inside his head hammers accusingly. "You've practically made Casey a single parent! And your daughter feels like she doesn't have a father!"

Two Are Better Than One

It seems fair to surmise that if someone could find a way to alleviate the problems that business travel creates for parents, that genius would become a wealthy individual in short order! But it can never be. For the reality of parenting is that children need their parents to *be there*—physically, emotionally, relationally, and spiritually.

We are not trying to add to anyone's guilt by pointing this out. It's just that kids need parents. Period! It's that simple. And a growing body of evidence supports that commonsense notion—along with the related idea that two parents are preferable to one. Kids need *both* a mom and a dad.

For example, Gene Stephens, a criminologist at the University of South Carolina, cites a Centers for Disease Control report that fatherless homes produce 85 percent of all children who exhibit behavioral disorders. Other research shows that fatherless children are 32 times more likely to run away, 9 times more likely to drop out of school, 10 times more likely to be substance abusers, and 20 times more likely to end up in prison.

Thus, when it comes to raising children, parents cannot just "phone in" their contribution. It has to be made in person, because that's what children are—*persons.* They demand (and deserve) a time-consuming, firsthand relationship with both Mom and Dad.

Does that mean travelers have no hope of ever developing intimacy with their kids and raising healthy children? By no means. *But it ain't easy!* It ain't easy for the obvious reason that travel takes them away—takes them out of their children's life *physically* and takes away the amount of *time* they have to spend with their kids relationally. Those are difficult obstacles to overcome.

And as if that were not enough, the absence of a parent affects more than the children; it affects the other parent—which is to say, it affects the traveler's marriage. We can see some of this in Jim and Casey's situation. The problems Jim's travel creates for his daughter, Madeline, spill over onto Casey. Casey doesn't exactly express it, but we suspect that her feelings toward Jim include some resentment, frustration, and disappointment because she ends up carrying the load of parenting all by herself.

We say that because we often hear travelers' spouses complaining about their mates' deficiencies as parents. "He runs off to the airport and leaves me with all the responsibility," a wife will say. "He has no idea what it takes to get the kids ready for school and on to carpool and after school to their activities and then back home and then dinner and then bedtime. And I have to go to work, too! Only I can't just pack a bag and walk away and say, 'Bye! See you next week!' I'm on duty twenty-four hours a day!"

Or a husband will complain, "I knock myself out to feed my kids and take care of them while their mother goes out of town, and you know what they want to know when I tuck them in at night? They say, 'Daddy, when will Mommy be home?' It's like she's the only one that counts! 'Where's Mommy?' And I'm thinking, 'Hey, what about me? I'm your father! I'm not just the nanny!'"

Given this reality, it's easy to see how business travel can affect a marriage through parenting by sapping the emotional strength of the parent at home. For instance, after spending herself on the care of the children all week, an exhausted wife may have little left to give when her traveling husband comes home, ready for romance. She may feel not only too tired for intercourse but resentful that her husband would even think of such a thing. "I've been putting up with these kids all this time, and all he can think of is coming home and jumping in the sack! Well, maybe if he gives me a day off and a long, hot bath and a good massage—then maybe I'll be ready to think about sex!"

Travelers and Their Children

It is impossible to generalize about the impact a parent's travel has on his or her children, as circumstances vary widely from family to family, and children respond quite differently. However, it is safe to say that any time a parent is absent, a child must come to terms with that absence. Needless to say, the child's imagination can be fertile ground for coming up with an answer as to why his or her parent is gone.

For example, one little boy, used to accompanying his mother when she dropped off his father at the airport, concluded that Daddy spent his entire time away on an airplane. The boy would look up in the sky, see a plane, and say, "Look! That's my daddy up there!"

On a darker note, a parent's repeated or prolonged absence can become internalized by a child in such a way that the child sees himself or herself as somehow the cause of that loss—especially if the parent provides no reassurances to the contrary. For example, an adolescent may come to the conclusion, "My mom goes out of town so much because she doesn't want to be around me." Likewise, the son of a performer who sees his father get "up" before going off to do a show and then sink into depression upon returning home may decide, "Dad loves being on the road, in front of a crowd, but he doesn't love me."

These messages, which may take years to form and may never be fully verbalized, can have a powerful impact on the youngster's self-concept. The issue is worth: "Where do I stand in my parent's estimation? How important am I to him or her? Do I matter?" In a child's mind—in anyone's mind—value is always measured in terms of time, attention, and concern. If a parent's time is consumed on the road and there is nothing left for the child, if the parent is preoccupied with matters of work and the child is ignored, if the parent gets concerned only about what happens outside the home and the interests of the child carry little weight—the child can only conclude, "I don't really matter." (It may be years—if ever—before the child is able to add a significant qualifier: "I don't really matter *to this person.*")

Again, there are ways to show time, attention, and concern despite the demands of heavy travel. *But it ain't easy!* It takes a lot more effort, which includes some careful planning and creative thinking.

The Disengaged Parent

We'll consider some of those plans and thoughts in a moment. But first, you should realize that travel can have as negative an impact on the traveling parent as it can on the traveler's kids. We've already pointed out the guilt the traveler may feel. We can add to this emotion a sense of estrangement as the traveler begins to feel isolated from his or her family, as if they were living in separate worlds.

For example, one traveler found himself avoiding phone calls home. "I hated to call and hear screaming kids in the background," he said. "It was like things seemed to be falling apart without me. They really weren't, but it sounded that way. And of course there was never anything I could do. So finally I started calling less and less—which actually made things worse at home."

It also made things worse on the road, because by not communicating with his family, that traveler felt cut off. He learned about events in the life of his wife and children days and weeks after the fact—long after he would have had a chance to take part in them, even at a distance.

Another effect travel has on parents is that it complicates their roles. Desmond was fairly involved in the life of his young son,

146

Dolphus, until he took a job with a large corporation. The new position required extensive travel, which caused quite a switch in Desmond's role as a father. His wife, Chantrelle, explained: "When he first started traveling, he would leave me and my boy, and we were pretty much on our own. Then just about the time we got comfortable, here comes Desmond, back into town. He'd just walk in and want to take over. And I'd be like, 'Look here! We got along just fine without you! Don't be handing out orders now that you're home!' Because I learned that in a matter of days he would be gone again, and we'd have to start all over."

This is a common reaction. When spouses at home must assume the majority of parenting responsibilities, they set up the household in ways that make the most sense for them. Understandably, they are loath to hand over control when the traveling spouse returns.

On the other hand, some travelers find it hard to reconnect with their families when they re-enter the picture. This relates to that sense of isolation they feel. When they walk in the front door, they sense that their partner has things under control, and they are reluctant to rock the boat. But that can lead to the ominous thought, "Gee, things seem to be going pretty well without me. Am I still needed?"

By now, you may be thinking that if travel can be hazardous to your marriage, it will be utterly perilous for your parenting. But there is a bright side worth mentioning. As difficult as travel can be for parent-child relationships, a traveler's longing to see his or her children helps to keep that traveler coming home. Absence does make the heart grow fonder. And if there's any consolation for the guilt that many traveling parents experience, it may be that feeling lousy about being away is not such a bad thing! It's a sign that home and family really do matter.

Is that true for you? If so, let's use that longing by implementing some practical strategies to offset the downside of your absence.

Parenting from the Road

There are so many ins and outs to the art of good parenting that we would be foolish to suggest any sort of step-by-step program for raising your children. Fortunately, there are many outstanding books on the market that delve into the finer points of parenting.

147

Our purpose is to offer suggestions pertaining to the challenges of raising a family in the midst of business travel. Much more could be said, but here are the highlights.

Pay Attention to the Impact of Travel

Come to terms with the impact travel has on you as a parent and on your children. Many of the parenting problems associated with business travel come from a far deeper problem: Too many travelers and their spouses don't pay enough attention to the effect travel has on their family. Often there is too much denial or too much apathy.

Our advice is to confront the issues head-on. Is your spouse furious because you are on the road and he or she feels stuck at home to do all the child rearing? If so, face that squarely. Is your teenage daughter or son like Madeline—wearing down the resistance of your partner at home, knowing that you are not there to reinforce the limits? If so, stop and take a look at that.

Only you and your family can decide what to do about the emotions, problems, conflicts, or troubles that stem from business travel. But you will never resolve those matters in a healthy way unless you admit they are there.

Along these lines, if you are the traveler, we urge you to come to grips with whatever guilt you may feel about being away from home. Accept the fact that some of that guilt is without foundation. After all, some jobs require travel; there's no way around it. So rather than look upon your trips as evil or wrong, consider them part of providing for your family, which is an expression of love and commitment. (Of course, as we've pointed out, sometimes the price may be too great to pay; then perhaps you need to find another way to make a living.)

In thinking about the impact business travel has on your family relationships, beware of blaming the road for problems that would be there with or without travel. For instance, a father who frequently came home after trips and physically abused his children used the excuse, "I just get so stressed out from traveling that I lose control." But there are many stressed-out travelers who don't abuse their children. So that behavior is not the result of travel.

Travel may contribute to it by creating stress, but the root of the problem lies elsewhere.

Establish a Parenting Structure with Your Spouse

When you and your spouse are separated by miles of real estate, it's a bit late to start worrying about things like communication, discipline, limits, rewards, accountability, values, and all the other parenting issues. The two of you need to work these out ahead of time so you have a game plan on which you both agree. That way, you present a united front to your children.

That's part of the reason why Madeline doesn't flinch when her mother declares, "Your father and I have made a rule. . . ." She knows her mom really means to say, "*I* have made a rule." Whatever authority her father exercises is by proxy, and he's not there to enforce it. This has been going on for so long that Madeline, at fifteen, no longer respects her mother's authority. While no one can predict exactly how a teenager will respond to authority, it seems fair to say that things might go differently were Casey able to say with conviction, "You know the rule. Your father and I have discussed it with you on more than one occasion. You have violated our agreement. Here are the consequences." Of course, Casey has to know that Jim will back her all the way.

This brings up the importance of setting expectations for your children's behavior ahead of time. They need to know what is acceptable when one parent (or even both) is away. If they sense that the rules change significantly as soon as Mommy or Daddy goes out of town, they will take advantage of the situation, making life miserable for the parent at home.

Address Your Children's Emotions

Your children's feelings—whatever they happen to be—express their reaction to their parent's going away. These emotions may seem unreasonable; they may make you uncomfortable. That's okay! Accept them for what they are, and listen to what they are telling you about your children.

Rules to Live By

Dallas Morning News columnist Steve Blow helps us face the responsibilities of parenting with his comments in a recent column, taken from an address he gave to a teachers' group. Steve doesn't believe our society has a crisis in education; he believes it has a crisis in *parenting.* "If we as parents were able to send happy, healthy, well-disciplined, and well-supervised children to school, there would be no crisis in education. Not that schools are perfect, but it might be time that we quit dumping everything on education and get honest with each other about the job we're doing as parents."

He goes on to say that maybe we ought to be holding ourselves to a higher standard of parenting. To help us do that, he offers twelve rules of responsible parenthood that are worth considering, whether we travel or not.

1. No R-rated movies.
2. Midnight curfew.
3. Go to church.
4. Turn off the TV.
5. Discipline well.
6. Get married, if you're not.
7. Stay married, if you are.
8. Say "no" sometimes (when saying "yes" will hurt them).
9. Say "yes" sometimes (when loosening up will strengthen the trust between you).
10. Teach respect.
11. Love abundantly.
12. Have fun.

Not a bad framework by which to run a household!

Steve invites comments at P.O. Box 655237, Dallas, TX 75265. If you don't agree with him, write him. But if you do, why not introduce this list into your family life?

This is so crucial for traveling parents to understand! If they only realized the value of letting their youngsters express how they feel about Mom or Dad being away. What an incredible opportunity to build a relationship!

Of course, it may not be easy. It can be a troubling thing to hear your seventeen-year-old daughter say, "Mom, you missed every softball game I played this season. I hated it, because all the other girls had their parents there!" But she is not necessarily saying that to hurt you. She is telling you something important about herself. What an honor that she would! That's what makes a relationship.

Keep Your Family Close to Your Heart

Taking steps to stay emotionally connected is the sort of thing you'd assume travelers and their families would automatically think to do. But they don't! So we offer this as a reminder.

Here are some questions for the traveler: Do you carry pictures of your family with you, perhaps in your wallet or date book? How recent are those photos? How often do you take them out and look at them when you're on the road?

The point is not to make you feel guilty if those photos are ten years out of date and collecting mold in the deep recesses of your wallet! The point is to encourage you to find a way to hold on to your family emotionally when travel takes you away. You don't want to succumb to the danger of "out of sight, out of mind."

Along these lines, we heartily encourage travelers to bring home gifts to their family. Not a bunch of overpriced trinkets from an airport curio shop! Gifts need not be expensive to be meaningful (although sometimes, when a trip has taken you away for weeks and months or caused unusual hardship on your family, something substantial is well in order).

Gifts ought to reinforce some connection between the one who gives and the one who gets. That's why a kid who collects rocks may be more impressed by a particular stone the parent found than he or she would be by a souvenir from a tourist stop. The stone says that the traveler genuinely had him or her in mind, had his or her interests at heart, had not forgotten either the child or what was important to the child. That's half the excitement about gifts from the road: They signify that the traveling parent was keeping his or her family in mind.

In a similar vein, it also helps to bring home gifts that are representative of the place the traveler has been. This escalates the value of the gift, in that it gives the family a snapshot of the traveler's journey, bringing the experience home to them, along with a sense of inclusion in the time away.

Meanwhile, the family at home needs to keep the traveling parent in mind, as well. "Out of sight, out of mind" can work both ways. One family avoided that by using a map to keep track of their father's travels day by day. Likewise, while his father was out of town, a teenager worked on a model sailboat, knowing that his father would be anxious to see the progress when he returned. That project was a way for the teenager to stay connected with his dad, even though hundreds of miles separated them.

Make the Most of Your Time Together

We've heard people complain about having to be away from their families, yet when they get home, what do they do? Head for the golf course, fill up their calendar with social events, spend all their time doing chores, watch TV.

If you really miss your family and wish you could be with them, *be with them when you're with them!* Go to your son's soccer game. Listen to your seven-year-old read a story. Sit and play the piano while your daughter sings. Get involved in your children's lives. *Be there for them!*

Again, that may mean that certain other things will fall through the cracks. Maybe the shrubs won't get clipped as often. Maybe the house will remain a little messier than it might have. Maybe you won't make it to your Sunday school class's swim party.

Can we speak freely? You'll have *lots* of time later on to get to those things. But you have, at best, eighteen years or so to spend with your children while they are still children—and a good portion of that time is taken up with travel. So what do you want to do with the days and hours remaining?

Think of Your Children When Scheduling Travel

Not everyone has the luxury of choosing when they will travel. But be proactive, not passive! If you have choices, if you can make your preferences known, if you have any say in when your travel takes place, take a look at your children's calendar and make an effort to book your trips accordingly. Try as hard as you can to be there for the important days and events in their lives (review chapter 8).

We're aware that some people, particularly in the corporate world and the military, feel pressure *not* to take family into

To Everything There Is a Season

"Being there" for your family is not the same as taking on certain "family-oriented" responsibilities—things like serving as a soccer coach, fund-raising for the PTA, volunteering at the YMCA, or teaching a children's Sunday school class. Those are important jobs, no doubt about it. But being there for your family means having a *relationship* with them. If you can do that and manage extra assignments—all the while fulfilling your work commitments—that's great.

However, in our experience, it's rare to find travelers with school-age children who can effectively do all that. Their time is already limited by having to be away. So when they come home, they need to give their children undivided attention. They don't need to dive into meetings and tasks that once again take them out of the home and away from their family.

This way of thinking may be contrary to the expectations of many people. But it's important to remember that life has many seasons. One of those is the season for raising a family. That's a time-intensive task, so parents in that season need to establish limits on outside commitments, to protect the time they have to spend with their kids. After all, opportunities to serve in the community will always be there, but your children grow up only *once.*

account as they take on work-related assignments. Somehow, considering their families supposedly displays weakness and complications that may come back to haunt them later when it comes to career advancement.

You'll have to decide what's most important to you. But decide and then act. Don't allow the machinery and agenda of the company to just roll over you and your family, as if you had no recourse.

Consider Taking Your Child on a Business Trip

Traveling with children can be a tricky juggling act and will not work for everyone, obviously. But by bringing your child along when you travel, you allow him or her to get a taste of what you experience as a business traveler. That may do more to help him or her understand you and what you face on the road than anything you could possibly say.

If you take a young child, you will have to find child care for the time when you are conducting business. And an older child must have something to do, as well, that is age appropriate. But if you can manage it—and if your employer has no objections—a shared trip can become a shared memory. It can open the door to lots of interesting things in your relationship. It can help to demystify travel—which is to say, demystify the traveler. For in the mind of every child whose parent must go away on business, the question always lurks: What is so important that my father or mother finds it necessary to leave me and go away?

12

All My Bags Are Packed and I'm Ready to Go

Saying Good-Bye

*O*ne of the classic scenes of motion pictures is the parting of people who are in love. Stop and think for a moment how many films include that poignant moment (often at the end of the movie) when two lovers wave good-bye as the train pulls out of the station . . . or embrace while the intercom announces the final boarding call of a flight . . . or break down in sobs as the taxi drives away. With the music swelling and the camera pulling back, viewers can't help but feel that ache of pathos that so often comes when people must say good-bye.

However, that's Hollywood. If you and your spouse are veterans of the business travel routine, we're willing to bet your partings aren't nearly so dramatic. (Indeed, we know a handful of people who are more than glad to see their spouses depart, and deserve an Academy Award just for *acting* as if they were sorry to see them go!)

In the next chapter, we'll consider the problems created by a traveler's "re-entry" into the home. The problems are much the same when a traveler is leaving. There's a certain tension in the air, and oftentimes a couple who really will miss each other find themselves at each other's throat just at the time when they "ought" to be feeling tender. Here's a case in point.

The Monday Morning Blues

Renée is sitting at the breakfast table, drinking coffee. Her husband, Colby, is back in their bedroom, packing for his trip to his company's annual employee convention. Renée would be willing to help, but experience has taught her to leave Colby alone when he is throwing things together to leave town.

Besides, on this morning she is fine about leaving him be. She did not sleep well, having tossed and turned all night, thinking about the previous evening.

On Sunday, Colby had gone off to play golf (which in itself caused her to be put out with him). He was supposed to have been home by 5:00. But it was not until 6:45 that Daniel, his golfing partner, had dropped him off. Colby had come through the door as if it were no big deal, shouting, "Hey, babe, I'm home! What's for dinner? I'm starving!"

"We already ate," Renée had said icily. "Dinner was ready an hour ago. I left some pizza in the oven."

Colby had paused for a moment as it began to dawn on him that his wife was none too happy. "Ooooo-kay!" he exclaimed hesitantly, then pushed past her to get some pizza.

She had followed him into the kitchen. "Why couldn't you have called?" she asked sharply.

"Hey, you know how it is on the golf course. Not a lot of phones."

"I thought Daniel carried a mobile phone with him?"

"Uh, yeah. Well, today, uh, I don't think he remembered to bring it."

"Is that it? Or did you not remember to ask him?"

"I don't know. Look, it wouldn't have made any difference. There were tons of people ahead of us on the course. You know how it is on a nice day like this."

"Yes, it *was* a nice day. And it would have been nice if your family could have spent it with you!"

"Aw, now, Renée—"

"I'm serious, Colby. Here you are getting ready to go out of town all week, and what do you do on the day before you leave? You run off to play golf with Daniel, who you see every day at work, and who you're going to see every day this week!"

"Yeah, but you see me every day, too."

"I do? I see you at six-thirty or seven every night after you've worked all day and you're too tired to talk. When you're in town, that is!"

Feeling stung by that barb, Colby had replied sarcastically, "Well, you could have seen more of me tonight—*if* you had waited to have dinner with me!"

Renée had rolled her eyes with a "what's the use?" look on her face. Frustrated that her "blockhead husband" didn't seem to "get it," she had turned on her heel and walked out of the kitchen.

The heat of the exchange had still been with her later as she tried to nod off to sleep. She had felt exhausted, but her mind kept churning angrily. Why Colby had to pick that day to go golfing was a mystery to her. It was true that Saturday had been rainy, so it had been the first real chance he had had to hit the links in quite a few weekends. "Still, he *is* leaving town," she kept thinking to herself. "Why didn't he spend that time with me and the kids?"

Thoughts like these had still been swirling when the alarm went off at 5:30. Colby had immediately jumped out of bed and headed for the shower. Renée had slowly dragged herself from under the covers and put on a robe and slippers. A few minutes later, she had gone to the kitchen. Soon she was listening to the gurgling of the coffee pot, rubbing her eyes, trying to wake up.

"Good-Bye to You, Too"

Now, after a few sips, Renée anticipates what will happen during the next hour. Sure enough, Colby finishes his shower and yells to her from down the hall, "Can you call the airport and check on the gate number for my flight?"

157

As she picks up the phone, she says to herself, "If he wakes those kids at this hour, I'll kill him!"

Meanwhile, Colby is a whirlwind of activity back in the bedroom. With practiced routine, he whisks clothes out of his closet, folds them neatly, and drops them into his suitcase. Socks, shoes, belts, underwear, and neckties follow. As he packs his shaving kit in the bathroom, Renée comes in with his flight information.

"Gate K-14." She pauses. "It's on time."

Colby doesn't respond but moves past her to his suitcase, making last-minute adjustments. From there he races to the kitchen. Renée follows a moment later and finds him rummaging through the refrigerator. "I don't really have time to eat," he is saying to no one in particular, "but I gotta find something, or I'll starve by the time I get fed on the plane. Besides," he adds as he pops a jelly roll into the microwave, "I can't stand airline breakfasts!"

The phone rings, and Renée picks up. "It's Daniel," she says, handing the receiver to her husband.

"Hey, guy, what's up?"

Colby spends the next few minutes on the phone. At first, it is evident that he and Daniel are working out some detail related to their trip. But then the conversation drifts to the previous day's golf game. There is lots of bragging and kidding.

Meanwhile, Renée is cursorily glancing at the headlines in the morning paper. But she can feel her anger rising. "Fifteen minutes before he has to leave," she is thinking, "and this is how he spends it—talking golf!"

Finally Colby signs off. "Boy, I gotta go soon," he says with a glance toward the clock on the microwave.

"I know," says Renée, with a mixture of frustration, resignation, and disappointment.

Colby heads for the den and sits down at his desk. He starts sifting through a stack of bills, pulling a couple aside to write checks. As he stuffs them into envelopes, he studies a third statement and calls out to Renée, "What's this big bill from the dentist's?"

"I took the kids to the dentist," says Renée, coming into the den.

"I know, but this is way too much. We can't afford care that costs this much."

Renée shrugs. "The kids had cavities."

158

"I know, but this is out of sight!" Colby shakes his head and starts to write a check. "Well, so much for eating out this month. We'll be in the poorhouse in short order if we have to keep paying bills like this."

"Yeah, well, you could always cut back on your golf."

Colby looks at her as if deeply insulted. "What's that supposed to mean?"

"It means what I said. You spend a lot of money on green fees and golf balls and what not. It adds up."

"I'll be the judge of that!" he snaps in a huff. Standing up, he goes over to the magazine rack and grabs the latest issue of *Golf Digest* and a *Sports Illustrated*. "I don't suppose you've seen my *National Geographic*," he mutters.

"Oh, we haven't gotten that in months. I didn't renew it. You never read it."

"You didn't renew it?!" he repeats incredulously. "You gotta be kidding! Thanks a lot!" Then, dropping the other two magazines in his briefcase, he looks up at her and says, "You don't know what I read!" He slams the briefcase shut and latches it with a definitive click. "I gotta go!"

Renée is waiting for him at the door to the garage after he goes back to get his suitcase. He is forced to pause as she gives him a routine hug in passing. "Will you call me when you get there?"

"Yeah, I guess so," he says moodily. "Say bye to the kids for me."

Renée watches him back out of the garage and pull away. As the garage door closes, she shakes her head, perplexed. "Good-bye to you, too!" she mumbles.

Stupid Little Tension Fights

The partings between you and your spouse may not be as chaotic and rocky as this one, but one thing is for sure: Departures by their nature tend to create stress in the home, producing tension that can flare up for seemingly no reason at all. As one wife of an Interstate Battery salesman put it, "We get into these little fights about stuff that doesn't even matter. It's not like we're really mad at each other. They're just stupid little tension fights."

That's a perceptive comment. If you and your spouse experience those kinds of petty conflicts around the time of departure, it might help to consider what's really going on. The squabbles probably have little substance in and of themselves. It's not that the points of contention—whether they are dentist bills, cancelled subscriptions, or whatever—are unimportant. But under ordinary circumstances, you would probably be able to negotiate these concerns in a fairly amicable way. Bring them up when the clock is ticking down to departure time, though, and you dump a load of tension into the mix. That can be explosive!

It's important to see this tension for what it is, because saying good-bye properly is crucial for your relationship. For one thing, a good-bye communicates value, affection, and support. It also provides reassurance. It's a final opportunity to check in with each other and ensure confidence, as if to say, "I'm okay about you. Are you okay about me?" Without that reassurance, a couple can feel profoundly uneasy all the time they are parted.

This helps to explain one of the recurring fears of many home-based spouses. If a couple has parted on a sour note, the spouse left behind worries that the traveler will die in a plane crash or other accident and the surviving spouse will be left without a sense of resolution or closure. That anxiety is born of the incredible void that is always left inside when someone leaves and there hasn't been a proper good-bye.

A similar feeling can grip the traveler. Without a proper send-off, he or she can feel mighty estranged, unwanted, or lonely. There can also be a lingering sense of guilt, and that can do a number on the traveler's effectiveness on the road. One man admitted that the worst trip he ever had came after he and his wife had engaged in a no-holds-barred argument in the car on the way to the airport.

"When we got to the airport, I jumped out of that car immediately! I thought, 'I can't get away from her fast enough.' I think she couldn't wait to get away from me, either, because she switched over to the driver's side and took off before I could even close the trunk!

"But I felt sick about that fight all through my trip. You know what the fight was about? Dog poop. That's right, dog poop! She was tired of the dog pooping all over her flower beds in the back

160

yard. Somehow, I found a way to make fun of that, and things went downhill. It was silly! But we were going at it.

"And it just ate away at me once I got away. I couldn't concentrate. I couldn't sleep. The worst of it was, I felt demoralized—just terribly ashamed of myself. I'd go in to meet with prospective clients, and I had this little voice in my ear, 'You jerk! You have nothing to offer these people. You can't even discuss dog poop with your wife intelligently.' It was like I had no right to be there.

"And you know what it really was? The whole thing was about needing her support. I needed to go out feeling that she was behind me one hundred percent. Instead, it was like we were enemies. I couldn't do my job that way."

And neither could his wife. For her, the issue was also about needing support. She needed him to hear her concerns about the dog poop and her flower beds. She was uncertain whether he cared about her concerns and whether he would do anything to remedy the situation.

Thus, like most arguments, this one was a two-way street and was about underlying issues, not just whatever instigated trouble in the first place.

The Experience of Loss

Why should departures wreak such havoc? Probably because they bring us face-to-face with the experience of loss, and most of us want to avoid that emotion if we can. You may not believe that is true for you, but don't be so sure. We humans are made to relate to one another, and as we have seen, few relationships are as significant as marriage. So when the time comes for our partner to suddenly go away, the reality of that separation can be painful.

There are different ways of defending against that pain. Some people deny it; some try to deal with it through humor. Some of us just swallow it, so we may not be in touch with our anxiety as the moment of parting looms. But stress has a sneaky way of leaking out. Irritability is one of those ways.

Of course, there are also some practical angles to the increase in petty conflicts that crop up around departure time. The twenty-four hours just prior to departure are often busy and demanding.

There are preparations to be made, chores to be done, lingering details to be cleaned up. All that can add to the schedule, which may already be packed. So the last-minute rush can place an imposition on the routine, and everybody is suddenly expected to "flex" to accommodate the traveler.

For example: Sharon has to be at the airport at 2:00. Her husband, Jim, is willing to drop her off, even though it means cutting short the time he would normally spend working on the yard. It also means that their daughter, Lauren, who has to be at a soccer game at 2:45, will have to ride along, which will rob her of time at home. And it means that the couple's toddler, Jason, must also ride along, so he won't get his nap, and he'll probably be a little cranky by dinnertime.

Not surprisingly, the trip to the airport is filled with tension. It ends up being a mad dash in which Lauren is yelled at for being late, Jason is crying about Mommy going away, Sharon is feeling hurried, and Jim is moodily pondering the load that is about to descend on him with his wife away. Is it any wonder that everyone is snapping at each other as the car barrels down the road toward the airport?

Parting Is Such . . . Sorrow

Have you ever considered the emotions associated with departure as a form of grief? The classic stages of grief include denial, anger, bargaining, depression, and acceptance. Many of us who travel extensively (or whose spouses do) have faced one or more of these feelings at one time or another. We may have become somewhat immune to them or more skilled at recognizing them and handling them. But next time you experience the tension associated with the separation of travel, consider whether you may be going through the very common experience of grief.

Learning to Soothe the "Ouch" of Good-Byes

Is there any way to surmount that sort of tension? Not really. At least, there's no easy way to do it. It's like going to the doctor to get a shot. When you're a child, you can't stand it. In fact, the apprehension that builds up as you approach the appointment almost becomes worse than the prick of the needle. The anxiety may gradually subside as one gets older. But the experience remains unpleasant; there's still an "ouch" to some extent. Certainly no one *enjoys* it.

In a similar way, none of us ever enjoys saying good-bye, even if we learn to tolerate it. It pricks our heart to some extent. For that reason, departure remains an unpleasant—or at least, less pleasant—part of travel.

Still, there are ways to cope with the "ouch" of good-byes. Here are a few suggestions.

Accept the Stress of Departure

If you feel lousy on the days when you or your spouse have to leave town, if you find yourself sad or depressed or angry or irritable, if you and your partner get into "stupid little tension fights," you may be thinking that there must be something wrong with you or your relationship. But guess what? In all likelihood, there's *nothing* wrong. You and your spouse are simply reacting as any normal people would to the stress of being parted. Recognize that and accept it for what it is!

Doing so can save you a lot of headaches. One couple routinely fought over when they needed to leave for the airport. He wanted to leave later; she wanted to leave earlier. This argument became so predictable that it took on the aura of a ritual that had to be carried out every time he was to leave town. Unfortunately, the husband interpreted these fights as a sign that his wife was trying to control him by making it so unpleasant to depart that he would be forced to curtail his travel.

Then this man came to see that the inevitable quarrel was just a way of blowing off steam. That helped him lighten up considerably. Indeed, the couple eventually turned this issue into a game in which they bet each other a dollar (the price of a toll road they took to the airport) on when they would actually arrive at the terminal. (Half the time he won; half the time she won!)

Develop Routines and Rituals

One way to manage (but not deny) the stress of departure is to organize the event by setting up an agenda of activities. This may involve a checklist of tasks that always need to be accomplished, such as writing checks, getting cash from the bank, watering plants, packing, and so on.

This idea may seem much too confining to some people, who thrive on the chaos of the last-minute rush. If that describes you, we don't want to cramp your style. But we challenge you to consider: Is your adrenaline-ridden approach acceptable to your spouse and family? Is it helping or hindering proper good-byes?

The advantage of a checklist is that it takes away some of the unknown, which is one source of the stress of departure. It ensures that the important things won't get overlooked, so the most important thing—saying good-bye—won't get overshadowed by a lot of frenzy.

Along the same lines, departures can be "ritualized" by making something special out of them. Have you ever been to a farewell party or a retirement banquet? Those are ceremonial ways of saying good-bye to someone. There's no reason why you and your spouse can't be creative and think up some ceremonies of your own to mark a departure.

For example, if one spouse is going to be out of town for a lengthy period of time—say, a week or more—why not have a special dinner with the family the night before he or she must leave? Or perhaps there's a special poem or prayer you and your partner can recite as you pull up to the terminal. Little rituals like these help to formally say the kinds of things that need to be said, such as, "The person leaving is important. He or she will be missed. The family will eagerly await his or her return." Wouldn't you want to have messages like these ringing in your ears as you head out on the road?

Prepare Contingency Plans

A lot of the battle around departure time is tactical. It involves details, plans, timing, and "the little things." As we all know, it's the little things that count. That's because oftentimes it takes only a small detail to create a big problem.

Yet having acknowledged that, we seasoned travelers know that Murphy's Law reigns when it comes time to go out of town. There are so many things that can go wrong—and it takes only one of them to really add to the stress of the moment.

The obvious way to defend against this added stress is to create backup systems in case the unexpected happens. For instance, What would you do if the car didn't start? Or you left your tickets on the side table by your front door? Or your three-year-old woke up with a fever? Or you got delayed by traffic? Or you couldn't find parking? Or they changed your departure gate?

You can't anticipate every contingency. And at some point, you have to learn to go with the flow. But you can avoid frying your loved ones with the heat of your tension and frustration by having a Plan B in case Plan A is disrupted.

Know What Your Spouse and Family Need

We can't tell you exactly how you should say good-bye to your spouse and family, because people differ greatly in their reaction to loss and separation. What is appropriate for one couple or family may not work for another.

Thus, you'll have to think about what you and your loved ones need when it's time for departure. In this regard, we suggest that you invite them to *tell you* what they need. Don't make assumptions. Find out what they would like to have happen or said or done in order for them to navigate the situation.

For example, Jim knows his family really desires his presence when a trip is looming. That's a sign of their love for him. Indeed, he takes it as a compliment that they want him around. Consequently, he makes an effort to spend extra time with his family in the days just prior to travel. He may cancel or postpone other commitments, and he tries not to schedule anything other than family time. That reassures them, and frankly, it's a comfort to Jim as well.

Jim doesn't like good-byes, so he drives to the airport on his own rather than have his family drive him, and he parks in the long-term lot. On the day he leaves, he and his family pretend that everything is as usual. He packs and loads the car, then checks the flight information. When it is finally time to go, he prefers not to make a big deal of it—just a simple, quick good-bye to Brenda and to his boys if they are home. Then he leaves. This seems to satisfy everyone's needs in the Coté family. Yet Jim will tell you that it took a while for them to figure that out. He's glad they did, however, because now it minimizes the tension for all concerned.

Make Home the Departure Point

This brings us to another suggestion: Consider making the point of departure the home rather than a public place. Sometimes it's easier on everybody to say your good-byes at the front door of your house rather than at a drop-off lane at the airport or in a busy train station. When you are in familiar surroundings, it's a lot easier to be sensitive to each other's needs. You don't have to endure prying eyes or the impatience of people waiting while you exchange affection.

Explore Loss in Your Family Background

Pay particular attention to this issue of saying good-bye if loss featured heavily in your background. For some people, good-byes go deep into the past. They tap into vast reservoirs of loss that these individuals may not even be aware of. Consequently, these folks may experience great upheaval around departure time. Some go to great lengths to avoid having to say good-bye to their loved ones.

For example, a woman who was orphaned as an infant developed migraine headaches every time her husband went out of town. Likewise, a man who grew up as a "military brat" and whose family relocated ten times by the time he was twelve had a tendency to leave town by traveling to the airport from his office and calling his wife from the departure lounge of the airport. Sometimes he connected with her, sometimes he didn't. But his good-byes were invariably brief and without passion—a habit that caused severe problems in the marriage.

If you have tendencies such as these or if loss and separation played a major role in your upbringing, you would be wise to explore these areas with your spouse and, we suggest, with a professional counselor as well. Departures caused by business travel have enough stress without the added burden of stirring up painful memories from your past.

Say Good-Bye

All the other suggestions are pointless if you never get around to saying good-bye. Yet believe it or not, countless travelers and their families either don't do this, or do it poorly.

Don't forget it! Just do it. Do it the best you can.

In a sense, every good-bye has a whiff of death about it. In fact, the word *good-bye* originally meant "God be with you." It's an expression of goodwill and, in effect, an admission that we live in a world of uncertainty. We want God to go with the person even if we can't. And this is a powerful sentiment. Indeed, how many times have you heard someone say about a departed loved one, "I wish I had told them good-bye"?

We don't mean to end this chapter on a morbid note. Quite the contrary. Saying good-bye is a way to seal ourselves into the heart of our loved one so wherever he or she goes, a part of us goes, too. By saying good-bye, we offer a blessing—the blessing of ourselves, the assurance that we are bound together with a love that will last forever.

What Did You Say
Your Name Was, Again?

Re-entry

*I*n the blockbuster movie *Apollo 13*, the drama of whether astronauts Jim Lovell, Fred Haise, and Jack Swigert will make it back from the moon in their crippled Apollo spacecraft builds to the climactic moment of re-entry, when the tiny command module passes through the earth's atmosphere. Communication goes "black" for several minutes, and the world holds its breath as all eyes and ears are trained on the Pacific, awaiting the crackling sound of a radio transmission and the glimpse of a parachute to indicate that all is well. Will the fragile vehicle survive the intense heat and stress created by the friction of re-entry?

A similar period of re-entry typically confronts business travelers and their loved ones when the traveler finally comes home. It's a time of expectation and hope—as well as stress and sometimes a bit of heat! Quite often, what was supposed to be a happy reunion suddenly turns sour, leaving everyone in a quandary as to what happened. As one salesman put it, "Somehow, when I get off that plane, I see all those faces smiling at me, and it's great! Then something happens. Before we're even out of the airport, we're all cross at each other! I hate it!"

Is that your experience? Let's look in on a couple whose re-entry mirrors this statement of disappointment.

"It's Good to Be Home (I Think)"

Mel has had a fantastic trip. As a regional sales manager for a real estate brokerage firm, he has visited local sales forces in five cities during a ten-day trip. All five are showing at least 20 percent higher sales this quarter. Why, several deals came together right during Mel's trip! He feels exhilarated by the success, although exhausted from the weariness of the road.

Now he is homeward bound. His plane is right on time into Colorado Springs, and he's looking forward to having his wife, Charlotte, and six-year-old daughter, Julie Ann, meet him. It will be so good to see them! On their way up to Aurora, the Denver suburb where they live, they'll stop for dinner, and Mel is thinking about all the exciting things he has to tell his family.

The plane pulls up to the gate. The passengers file out (taking forever, it seems). Finally Mel's turn comes, and he strides up the Jetway. Coming into the terminal, he scans the crowd, looking for Charlotte's captivating smile and Julie Ann's outstretched arms as her little legs race to greet her daddy.

But there are no familiar faces at the gate. Mel stands there for a moment, watching other passengers meeting their loved ones. An attractive couple are embracing. A toddler squeals with delight as his grandparents arrive, gifts in hand. A father and a teenager welcome the family's mother. But no one is there for Mel.

Finally he realizes he is obstructing other passengers trying to deplane, and he shuffles off to retrieve his luggage. "Maybe they got delayed," he thinks. "Maybe they were late parking the car and just decided to meet me at baggage claim. Not the usual procedure, but anything's possible."

Baggage claim is a madhouse. Several planes have arrived at once, and it's forty minutes before Mel grabs his second bag from the carousel. Not that he's in a hurry. Charlotte is nowhere to be found.

Mel walks back toward the gates, wondering if he and Charlotte have simply missed each other. But with each passing moment, it becomes apparent that something is amiss. Mel calls home, but just gets the answering machine. Charlotte is not at home. She must be on the way.

"Sorry!"

Indeed she is on the way. She is racing down I-25, having completely forgotten Mel's arrival. She had invited her sister, Cheri, to visit, and the two of them had become lost in conversation. Only when Cheri asked her what time Mel was getting home did Charlotte realize how late it was.

"Oh, my goodness! We should have left an hour ago!" Charlotte exclaims as she jumps up and starts throwing herself together. Soon they are speeding south, chatting with nervous energy. This conversation manages to siphon off some of Charlotte's anxiety about being late, so when they arrive at the Colorado Springs terminal, she is actually laughing about the situation.

Unfortunately, Mel is in a very different mood. He's had about forty-five minutes to sit and stew over his wife's tardiness. He's collected quite a few choice thoughts to lay on her when she finally arrives.

But when he sees their car pulling up and heads outside, he realizes that someone else is in the car with Charlotte. When Charlotte opens her door and the interior light comes on, he can see who it is. His heart drops even lower. He and Cheri do not get along well. "It's going to be a long ride home," he thinks.

"Sorry!" Charlotte is saying as she runs around the car to embrace him. "I messed up the time! Cheri's in town, and we got talking. I'm sorry you had to wait."

"Yeah, well . . . so am I," Mel mumbles. Suddenly the eloquent tongue-lashing he intended to deliver has lost its energy, and the words have evaporated from his mind.

The threesome make small talk as Mel drives back to I-25. As they accelerate onto the highway, Mel raises the prospect of dinner.

170

"I'm not really hungry," Cheri replies.

"Yeah, we had a big lunch, honey," Charlotte explains. "But if you want something, you can stop someplace."

Mel thinks this over for a moment. "That's okay. I'll just grab something at home."

"I don't know what you'll have. I didn't go to the grocery store today, like I usually do. I have to go tomorrow. But there's probably something in the freezer."

Now Mel is wishing he had eaten at the airport. "Where's Julie Ann?" he asks.

"Oh, she's spending the night at a friend's house. She said to say hi."

A few moments of silence pass, and then Cheri starts talking. Soon she and Charlotte are chatting away. Mel does not feel like entering into the conversation. He is tired, hungry, and wondering why he feels so grumpy. He reminds himself what a good trip it was, but somehow the experience no longer has the same shine. It's as if the disappointments of his arrival have negated the exuberance of his travels. He no longer wants to talk about what happened on the road. He just wants to get home.

Then, as he heads into the blackness north of the Air Force Academy, he notices that the gas tank is nearly empty.

The Reconnection

There are many factors that can contribute to a rough re-entry other than a late pickup at the airport: late planes, lost baggage, bad weather, missed flights, just to name a few. We've heard of travelers showing up intoxicated, greeters being sent to the wrong terminal by airline employees, cars breaking down on the way to and from the airport. We've been told of the major problems caused by the family scheduling an important event on the evening of the traveler's return, by travelers being handed a list of duties they are expected to perform now that they are home, even by travelers landing at the wrong airport!

There are a thousand possibilities for breakdowns and letdowns when it comes to coming home. The question is *Why?* Why should re-entry be so prone to foul-ups and disappointments? After all, it's the moment most travelers and their loved ones look forward to with the greatest expectations. If anything about a business trip should go right, it should be the reunion. Yet so often, that's the part that goes wrong. How can that be?

The answer is fairly obvious when you stop to consider the nature of re-entry. It's the point at which two people—or several people, in the case of a family—are coming back together and must get reacquainted. It stands to reason that there's liable to be friction and misunderstanding, because the traveler is coming from the road and the loved ones are coming from home—two very different places. Both parties will have to readjust.

The touchdown of a plane serves as a useful analogy. Here is a fully loaded jetliner coming in at about 165 miles per hour. Its tires, which are of course going 0 miles per hour, dangle inches above the runway. Then rubber and concrete connect. When the motionless wheels hit that rough, immovable surface, there's a screech and some heat and even smoke as a bit of rubber burns off and the wheels start spinning. That's what it takes for tires to go from 0 to 165 miles per hour instantaneously.

In a similar way, it's not always easy for a returning traveler and his or her spouse and family to get up to speed with one another. Their agendas, expectations, and needs can be enormously different. It's not an issue of selfishness; it's an issue of different perspectives.

We saw that in the case of Mel and Charlotte. Mel was all excited and wanted to celebrate his successful trip by having dinner with his family. He wanted a chance to crow about the good things that happened. He hoped his wife and daughter would cheer his good fortune, thereby validating him as a competent worker, an adequate provider, and a worthy person. There was nothing wrong with that desire. But unfortunately, circumstances at home precluded it from being fulfilled.

That's because Charlotte also has a life. She was enjoying time with her sister. And while she would admit she was remiss in letting the time get away from her, she did nothing fundamentally wrong. Indeed, in a way, Mel's return actually interfered—or at least competed—with Charlotte's plans. Charlotte would have just as soon spent the evening in conversation with her sister. Her mind was not on real estate deals in other cities. She wanted to talk with her sister about important matters—and not-so-important matters, too. Basically, she just wanted to talk with her sister.

It's not that Charlotte wasn't glad to have Mel home. She was very glad of it. In fact, she was hoping to have some good, long talks with Mel too. But when she showed up at the airport in Colorado Springs, she wasn't hungry, she wasn't feeling lonely, she wasn't expecting to hear tales of commercial transactions. She was just glad to have Mel back.

It will take a while for Mel and Charlotte to get up to speed. There are things they can do to make that transition easier—or harder, if they so choose. But they, just like you, cannot get around the fact that reconnecting after business travel usually involves some stress. (We should point out that even couples whose work does not require travel often go through the momentary stress of re-entry every day when one or both partners arrive home from work.)

Why Re-entry Creates Tension

You and your spouse will want to consider why your re-entries may often be fraught with tension. But we suggest four ways in which a traveler's return can produce heat and smoke in the marriage.

1. Reunions Provoke Feelings about the Status of a Relationship

Imagine a traveler on the road for several days. The pace has been hectic. The traveler's mind and emotions have been focused on the tasks at hand. Home and marriage have been pushed to the background. But now, the traveler is sitting on a return flight and instinctively becomes conscious once again of the person waiting at the other end.

Is that spouse someone the traveler still looks forward to being with? Is the marriage satisfying and productive, or disappointing and possibly even destructive? Will the spouse be glad to have the traveler home? What sort of welcome can the traveler expect? What sort of problems await? What unfinished business is there to deal with? What hopes are there for the future? What plans does the traveler expect to pursue with his or her partner? What commitments must be fulfilled? How does the traveler feel about going home?

173

Meanwhile, the person at home may be reviewing the nature of the relationship, as well. While the traveler was away, the spouse was likewise preoccupied with his or her routine, going through each day without thinking much about the traveler. Now that person is coming home. Is that good or bad? Is the home-based spouse looking forward to the re-entry with anticipation or contemplating it with dread? Or perhaps he or she feels ambivalent about the reunion—not particularly moved one way or the other. In any case, what will the return of the traveling spouse mean? What changes will be called for? What possibilities will open up? Are there things that the home-based spouse needs to tell his or her partner? Is there news that will affect their marriage?

Who knows the extent to which questions like these actually enter into consciousness? But they are there, and the prospect of re-entry helps bring them near, if not to, the surface. That's normal and healthy. Indeed, if questions like these are not asked at some level, you have to wonder about the integrity of the marriage. You can't really say you have much of a relationship if, having been separated from your spouse for a period of time, you don't have at least some feelings about getting back together!

Couples who have healthy marriages inevitably have some feelings as they reconnect from travel. The re-entry process tends to

Houston, We Have a Problem

Think for a moment of some of the difficult re-entry experiences you and your spouse have had. In which areas were you feeling stress? Jot down a few thoughts right now, and make note of some of the reasons—as you perceive them—why strain and tension might have been provoked.

This exercise will be useful when we look at some of the remedies for re-entry problems later. It can also be a significant first step toward elevating intimacy in your marriage and dispersing some of the natural tension related to the challenge of re-entry.

bring out those feelings. If a couple is wise, they will let the process play itself out, and grow deeper in their relationship.

2. Returning Travelers Need Time to Regroup

When a company puts a person on the road, it does so with high expectations. It is not sending the individual on a vacation; whoever is paying for the trip expects results. Thus, business travelers tend to have their game face on when they are on the road. They often ride an adrenaline high, getting themselves up for their work-related challenges (no doubt, some are addicted to adrenaline—a serious problem to which travelers and their employers ought to pay attention).

But when the traveler finally heads home, there's an inevitable letdown. Depending on a number of factors, this can vary from a mild sense of slowing down, of unwinding, to a serious crash, the traveler crumbling emotionally and battling a strong bout of depression.

Whatever the nature of the traveler's decompression, it can be hard for a spouse at home to relate to. Why the moodiness, why the terse responses, why the lethargy and sudden lack of motivation? The answer is, Because the traveler has been up for days on end. Now it's time to let down, to rest and regroup.

Unfortunately, too many travelers, whether by choice or circumstance, fail to adequately regroup before they return to the pell-mell rat race of their work. If they keep that up, they will become prime candidates for burnout. What's worse, their loved ones will keep getting the leftovers, and their relationships will suffer greatly.

3. Re-entry Forces a Couple to Face Reality

Re-entry reminds both the traveler and the at-home spouse of all the things left undone before and during the trip. These may be tangible things, like chores waiting to be completed, or emotional issues, like unresolved conflicts.

For example, Lester has been "baching it" all week while his wife was out of town. He's basically let the apartment become a wreck. His intention was to come home after work and straighten

175

up enough to make the place look presentable. But his wife calls him at work and tells him she's been able to book an earlier flight; can he come right from work and pick her up? He can hardly say no. So for the rest of the afternoon, Lester sweats out what his wife is going to say when she finally arrives home to find . . . an absolute mess! Needless to say, re-entry for him probably will not go as well as it could have.

Or take the case of Marsha, who has the train ride from Washington, D.C., to New York to think about how she left things with her husband, Sam. It was not a pleasant parting. He wants to buy a particular set of audio speakers—a *very* expensive set. She wants to put the money into savings. They picked the morning of her departure to discuss (fight about) this decision. He left for work in a huff. She packed quickly, unusually energized by her anger. "It'll be too soon before I see that man again!" she muttered to herself as she locked up and left.

But now she can't wait to get home. Only, she knows Sam will be there when she arrives. They haven't spoken on the phone for the past three days. What is she going to say? How is he going to respond? How are they going to patch up this squabble?

There is no getting around the fact that travel is an escape. It allows you to literally walk or drive or fly or sail away from the less-pleasant matters of life—particularly the responsibilities, commitments, and conflicts of marriage. But sooner or later, it's time to come home—which means it's time to face that which you would just as soon ignore. Could that have anything to do with why re-entry is often so stressful?

4. Reunions Can Produce Unfulfilled Expectations

Even the best marriage can experience tension upon re-entry when either partner's expectations are unfulfilled. Often the reason for these disappointments is poor communication.

Recall the incident between Charlotte and Mel. Perhaps things would have gone better if Mel had called home the night before his return and suggested to his wife that the family go out to dinner when he arrived. That way, Charlotte would have had an opportunity to mention that her sister was paying an unexpected visit and that perhaps it would be best to postpone those dinner plans. Mel's plans still would have been altered, and he still might have felt disappointed. But at least he would have known what to expect. And of course, that phone call could have reminded Charlotte of his arrival time.

Hitting the Window

In *Apollo 13*, navigating a successful re-entry required the astronauts to maneuver their capsule to hit the atmosphere at just the right angle. Too steep, and they would burn up like a meteor. Too shallow, and they would skip off the atmosphere, dooming themselves to drift forever in the vast emptiness of space. Everything depended on hitting a narrow window of re-entry.

As you and your spouse maneuver to negotiate a successful re-entry from business travel, here are some practical suggestions to help you hit the window. These are tips offered by seasoned travelers and their spouses, who have learned that the only thing harder than having to be apart can be the strain of coming back together.

Accept As Normal the Stress of Re-entry

There's no getting around it. Re-entry is a time of expectations and tension. You can't eliminate that stress; you can only try to ameliorate it. The more you acknowledge the reality of re-entry, the more prepared you'll be to expect the unexpected.

Defend against Problems by Planning

As always, the best defense is a good offense. A lot of problems can be avoided simply by good planning and clear communication. For example, here is a brief checklist of things you and your spouse should remember every time business travel forces you apart.

A Re-entry Checklist for Travelers

Write down pertinent travel information, such as the arrival time and flight number of the traveler's return flight.

Write down the name and phone number for where the traveler will be staying and where the other spouse will be if not at home.

Write down names and phone numbers where you will leave messages if you can't reach each other.

Discuss plans for the day of, the evening of, and the day after the traveler's return.

Have the traveler call home just before returning, to confirm arrival details, discuss any last-minute changes in travel plans, get a feel for the situation at home, and convey his or her expectations.

If the home-based spouse is to pick up the traveler (for example, from an airport, train station, bus depot), does that spouse need to call ahead to check details like arrival time and gate number?

Many of the problems couples experience in re-entry boil down to small details they have overlooked. As we've said, re-entry is already a time of stress, so it doesn't take much to upset the apple cart. Conversely, with a little planning, things can often go quite well.

As the checklist indicates, be sure to extend those plans beyond just the day of re-entry. The eighteen to twenty-four hours immediately following the traveler's return are crucial. That's the period of re-adjustment. So it makes sense to consider what is and is not on the schedule during that period.

At Interstate Battery, the salesmen usually arrive home on Friday nights. Come Saturday morning, what do you suppose they want to do? Hit the golf course! What do their wives want to do? Go shopping! One small problem: Who is going to watch the kids? "I've had them all week; it's your turn!" say the wives. "I've had a hard week; I've got to unwind!" reply the husbands. It's a classic conflict in the making!

Can you see how some planning on Friday night—or even earlier in the week—might avoid misunderstandings and hard feelings? Working together, a couple can anticipate problems and negotiate a workable compromise. They can recognize that both of them have needs—brought on in part by travel—and find ways to ensure that their needs are met.

Keep Things Flexible during Re-entry

Don't accept a dinner invitation an hour after the plane is supposed to land. Don't promise your four-year-old, "Daddy's going to take you to a movie just as soon as he gets home." Don't put a roast in the oven and time it to be done precisely when the shuttle drops your spouse at the door. In other words, don't make any plans contingent on the traveler's schedule. There are too many unpredictables.

A salesman named Charley "Tremendous" Jones used to talk about "flexibility planning." Always plan for things to go wrong, he said. That way, you'll be prepared. And if they should go right? You can always work that in!

A word here about children. It's just inevitable that young children are liable to misbehave around the time of re-entry. For one thing, kids have a way of tuning in to tension and then translating that into behavior. So after you've scooped up your child and thrown him or her into the car and dashed to the airport and rushed through the terminal to pick up your spouse, don't be surprised if he or she pitches a fit right there in the concourse. As a child, he or she is simply doing what a lot of us adults would secretly like to do: Let out all our tension by throwing a tamper tantrum.

Furthermore, children naturally want attention when Mommy or Daddy gets home. They've been without their parent for a while. Their parent walks in. What else can we expect but that they assume that Mommy or Daddy is now there *for them?* So they hog the show! Our advice is to pay them the attention they so richly deserve. You can get into substantive conversation with your spouse and teenagers later. But for the first few minutes, allow little Johnny or Suzie that instant gratification so essential to their sense of security. One thing's for sure: You won't get very far with anyone else *until* you pay them some attention!

One final reality that makes re-entry so difficult for children is that so often it occurs late in the afternoon, when their bodies are low on food. So plan ahead. If you're going to be waiting at a terminal around dinnertime, fix a baggie of cereal or trail mix and bring along some juice. You might also carry a bag of small toys and games to keep small children from getting bored, especially if there's a delay.

Attach Traditions to the Process

One way to relieve some of the stress and tension of re-entry is to build little rituals into the occasion. It may be as simple and silly as letting your toddler ride on your shoulders as soon as you arrive and are headed toward baggage claim. It may be whistling a tune or reciting a ditty that has meaning for you and your spouse. It may be throwing a penny toward the runway to mark your return. The point is, let a little humor and whimsy off-load some of the stress of getting home.

One family established a tradition of having pizza for dinner whenever their traveling father returned from a trip. This was a flexible and easy meal to prepare, and a dish the whole family enjoyed. Consequently, the term "pizza night" came to be associated with the father's return. It was something to look forward to. In fact, on one occasion, when asked to spend the night at a friend's house, one of the traveler's sons replied, "I can't. Tonight's pizza night!" What he was saying was that his father was coming home—and he had no intention of missing it!

Clearly Communicate Your Expectations

Here we are, back to the issue of communication! As always, it is a key dimension of marriage. It is certainly crucial at the time of re-entry.

If there's something you need, you must let your spouse know what it is. If there's something bothering you, let it out. If you're hoping for things to go a certain way, be clear about what you want. The more you communicate your expectations, the smoother the transition is likely to be from the road to home.

For example, consider the mother who is tending a sick toddler at home while her spouse is away for several days. If she's wise, she will let her husband know that little Janie is throwing up . . . that she herself is feeling lousy, having been up all night running the child to the bathroom . . . that she's been unable to take his shirts to the cleaner, as she had intended . . . that the house has not been cleaned in a couple of days.

In short, this woman would be wise to communicate the reality of her situation. Otherwise, upon his return, her hubby is liable to pull into the driveway with his own set of expectations, only to have them dashed as soon as he opens the door. It's not as if she owes him an explanation. It's not as if he can't be flexible about his plans. It's just that re-entry—which is by nature a powder keg of stress—might go a whole lot smoother if the husband understands ahead of time how things stand.

Make Home the Re-entry Point

For travelers who use public means of transportation, one way to eliminate some problems (although it may create others) is for the traveler to find his or her own way home from the airport, bus depot, or train station, and have the reunion at home rather than in a crowded terminal. That interval between the arrival gate and the front door may give the traveler more time to catch his or her breath and calm down from the tension of traveling back.

Furthermore, public spaces can create tension all their own. If you've ever sat in a crowded, stuffy lounge with someone's colicky infant wailing on and on—or worse, if you've ever tried to calm your own colicky infant while sitting in a crowded, stuffy lounge with people listening to your baby wail on and on—you understand what we mean! Experiences like that don't exactly put you in the best frame of mind. Wouldn't you rather be less stressed out when you finally greet your loved one?

And then there's always the chance that in a public place, you will meet someone just at the moment when you intended to— and need to—focus on your loved one. Both of us have had occasion to get off a plane after a long trip, eagerly anticipating a reunion with our wives, only to discover that someone we know is meeting a party on the same flight. It's awkward because you want to be sociable and polite, but frankly, you'd rather just be alone with your spouse! But no, you find yourself having to make small talk at the baggage claim area, wondering if you'll ever be able to collect your luggage, say good-bye to the acquaintance, and—*at last!*— get out to the car and have some privacy with your mate.

One way to avoid all that is by grabbing some other means of transportation home and making your front door the point of re-entry. It's always easier to deal with stress when one is in familiar surroundings, and nothing could be more familiar than home. It may be a lot easier to reconnect with your loved ones when you turn your key in the lock, open the door, and hear those wonderful words: "You're home!"

There's No Place Like Home

I find this to be best for my household. The way I manage my energy to achieve business results finds me still working to complete my trips while I'm at the airport. I don't feel like I've finished my job until I pull into my neighborhood. Thus the one-hour trip from the airport to my home helps me make an adjustment back into my city and into the atmosphere that I'm used to. It also prepares my attitude for the intimate relationships I enjoy at home. So I highly recommend that you use the interval between the arrival gate and the front door of your house to catch your breath and calm down as you re-enter your family's world.

Jim Coté

14

Where's the Center?

Building a Spiritual Foundation

*N*o doubt you have walked or driven by a construction site where workers have recently broken ground to put up a building. What's the first thing they do? Logic would suggest they immediately start piling up steel and concrete. But in fact, they do just the opposite. Instead of building up, they start digging *down*. Before a single truckload of building materials is ever brought in, countless truckloads of dirt are *hauled out*. Indeed, half the time that it takes to put up a building may be spent on the foundation. It's a part that will never be seen once the building is up, yet it's the part on which everything else will rest.

Couples who want their marriages to be built strong and tall also need to establish a solid foundation. They need to sink, as it were, relational pilings deep down into spiritual bedrock, anchoring their union on a firm platform that will prove steady and secure amidst the forces that inevitably come against a marriage relationship.

The Longing Within

More and more people today are coming to this realization. They read about divorce rates that are skyrocketing. They hear "experts" questioning the institution of marriage itself. Many have firsthand experience of a relationship that is teetering precariously or perhaps has already buckled and crashed to the ground. And they wonder, "How can I keep this from happening to me? How can I and my spouse stand tall against the stresses and strains that seem to want to pull us down and pull our marriage apart?"

We believe that the answer to this question is to build a strong spiritual foundation for one's marriage relationship. Deep in the heart of every person is a need or longing for a sense of meaning and purpose, a sense that there must be more to life than just going to work in order to make money in order to buy things in order to enjoy an affluent lifestyle. As humans, we seek something deeper than that, something that connects with the core of who we are, something that lends significance to our lives, something transcendent or eternal.

Bookstores stock numerous titles promising ways to satisfy that quest for the spiritual. But routinely overlooked in these discussions is the fact that if you are married, your spirituality is inseparably linked to that of your spouse. Think about it! Here you are, with all your hopes and fears, capabilities and needs, thoughts and feelings, attractions and turnoffs—and right there beside you is your mate, with all of his or hers. How could the two of you possibly not affect one another at the deepest and most profound levels of your being?

In his powerfully thought-provoking book *The Mystery of Marriage,* Canadian writer Mike Mason points out that socially, legally, physically, emotionally—however you want to look at it—there is no other means of getting closer to another human being than by marrying that person.

> Everywhere else, throughout society, there are fences, walls, burglar alarms, unlisted numbers, the most elaborate precautions for keeping people at a safe distance. But in marriage, all of that is reversed. In marriage the walls are down, and not only do the man and woman live under the same roof, but they sleep under the same covers. Their lives are wide open. . . . A man and a woman face each other across the breakfast table, and somehow through a haze of crumbs and curlers and mortgage payments

they must encounter one another. That is the whole purpose and mandate of marriage. All sorts of other purposes have been dreamed up and millions of excuses invented for avoiding this central and indispensable task. But the fact is that marriage is grounded in nothing else but the pure wild grapplings of soul with soul, no holds barred (p. 74).

Recent years have brought a spate of books, seminars, video series, and other resources for dealing with these "grapplings of soul with soul." Many of these have much to recommend them. For our part, though, we find the most helpful perspective on this issue coming from traditional Christianity. This means that along with millions of other Americans, we believe that a couple grows closer together as they grow closer in relation to God.

Let us be clear. We're not saying that you have to be a Christian to have a solid marriage. Nor are we saying that if you and your spouse are "religious," you will automatically have a healthy and satisfying relationship. What we are saying is that couples who want a strong, lasting marriage inevitably pay attention to the spiritual dimension of their life together. As Christians, we and our spouses do that in the context of our Christian faith. We find there an enduring tradition that honors marriage and offers abiding truths and precepts that act as a bedrock on which to build our marriage relationships.

Admittedly, spirituality is a difficult topic for many people to discuss, living as we do in this deeply secular age. But there's no getting around the fact that the quest for meaning is probably the central driving force in life. So along with communication, commitment, finances, and all the other aspects of marriage affected by business travel, we might as well look at the spiritual dimension. Perhaps your experience of this issue will parallel that of Philip and Annie, who have a basically good marriage yet instinctively feel they need something more.

The Invitation

It's Saturday evening. Philip and Annie are sitting down to dinner with their young children. Philip is still feeling tired after arriving home the previous night from a week on the road, selling pharmaceuticals.

After Annie dishes out the food and helps the children get settled, she turns to her husband. "Phil, I was wondering . . ." she begins.

A mildly pained expression forms on Philip's face, as if to say, "Now what?"

Annie continues. "I was on the phone with Maggie this week, and she asked if we'd like to go to church with her and Steve tomorrow."

Annie pauses, looking for some reaction. But Philip just chews on his food.

"You know, they go to that big church over in Oak Bluff. Maggie says the minister there is a really good speaker. He's funny and he's interesting and he doesn't turn people off. And she says they've got great music and stuff—it's not real 'churchy.' Anyway, I guess tomorrow they're having some special program. I thought maybe we could take the kids."

"Is that where Caitlin goes?" asks Lucy, their six-year-old daughter. Lucy's playmate Caitlin is Maggie's daughter. "She's always talking about Sunday school and how fun it is. Can we go, Daddy, can we?"

Philip sighs. "I don't know! I'm so tired. You know, I'm on the road so much, and Sunday is one of my few days off. Besides, if you want me to fix that garage door, Annie—"

"Garage door! That's been broken for weeks! And you usually play golf on Sundays, anyway. Couldn't we go to church just this once? I don't think we've been since your folks were here right after Lucy was born. You'll have all afternoon to fix the garage door—or golf, for that matter!"

Philip shakes his head. "You know how I feel about churches, Annie. I just don't trust them."

There is a great deal of history behind this comment. The fact is that Philip's family attended church regularly while he was growing up. He had been active in Sunday school and youth programs. In fact, when he was preparing to graduate from high school, the preacher at his church told Philip that he should consider a career in the ministry.

"You have good communication skills," the pastor said, "and I notice that other kids look up to you. You're a leader. You have a real talent for persuasion. That could be a powerful asset if you pursued the ministry."

But Philip had no interest in becoming a minister. Indeed, when he went off to college, he never attended church and more or less let his faith lapse. Not that he ignored the spiritual side of life. Many a late-night bull session in his dorm centered on metaphysics and deep philosophical questions. And as an adult, he still occasionally reads books like Scott Peck's *The Road Less Traveled*, or Robert Fulghum's *All I Really Need to Know I Learned in Kindergarten*, or something by C. S. Lewis.

Of course, Philip and Annie had been married in a church. And family funerals were held there. But beyond that, Philip had come to have little use for organized religion.

Searching for a Center

"Maybe you and the kids should go," Philip suggests to his wife, hoping that this will be an acceptable compromise.

Annie frowns. "That's no good! There I'll be, with Steve and Maggie, and everyone will be looking at me like, 'Where's her husband?' I don't want that! Besides, this church is supposed to be a church for families."

Philip sighs, as if he may be weakening. "I don't know." He chews for a moment. "You know, you visit one of these churches, and next thing you know, they're pitching you to join. I remember at my church growing up, they had a whole committee that did nothing but go out and try to convince visitors to come back and join the church. I mean, it was *organized!*"

"I know," Annie replies, "but maybe this will be different. Hey—Steve and Maggie go, and you like them. They're not, like, pushy or anything about their religion. I mean, Maggie just mentioned this program they're having and thought we might enjoy it. She even said, 'Tell Philip he can be out the door by noon and on the links by twelve-thirty!'"

Philip smiles sheepishly.

"Anyway," Annie goes on, "I've been thinking that—well, I'd like to see us bring God into our family more. You know what I mean? I mean, the kids certainly need it. And I look at Steve and

Maggie and their kids, and it just seems like they have a certain, uh, center or something to their family. I don't know how to explain it. They just seem like—well, like they have something there that I'd kind of like to see in our family. Somehow I think religion has something to do with it. Maybe it doesn't, but I guess I'd like to find out more."

Philip pauses, reflecting on Annie's words. He knows exactly what she means, because he's been feeling some of the same things himself. He just hasn't brought it up, because the whole subject seems a bit too threatening. After all, when it comes to religion, who knows where things might lead? But now that Annie has spoken, he actually feels relieved. Maybe Steve and Maggie's church will have a new slant on things, maybe it won't. But at least it's a way to explore the issue.

"Maybe you're right," he finally says. "I'll tell you what. Let me get a decent night's sleep, and then let's decide in the morning. Okay?"

Annie smiles and nods.

The Tie That Binds

There is no guarantee, of course, that Philip and Annie will find what they are looking for at Steve and Maggie's church. But they are moving in the right direction by talking about the need for a "center" to their marriage and family life and by seeking a way to create that spiritual bond.

This is a wise move, given the fact that our society is pulling couples and families apart as never before. Consider the many forces and factors that, intentional or not, manage to estrange husbands from wives, and parents from children: overburdened schedules, messages from the entertainment industry, high mobility, the growing prevalence (and necessity) of two incomes to support a family, the stresses generated from other societal institutions such as the schools and the workplace. Unless the members of a family share a common loyalty to a set of beliefs, values, and traditions that uphold their family life, they will be sorely pressed to renege on their commitments to one another—or, at the very least, to be confused about the many choices offered them.

188

Thus, spirituality serves as a cohesive force in marriage and family life. It allows parents, for example, to point out to their children that while others may follow a different set of standards, "our family does it this way, and this is why." Likewise, a couple may use their convictions about the meaning of their relationship as a basis for saying no to a certain career opportunity that comes along, because, attractive as the offer may be, it would sacrifice the quality of their relationship.

To outsiders, this spiritual center can seem odd and, at times, limiting. A news reporter for one of the major networks tells of the strange looks colleagues who are divorced sometimes give when this reporter declines additional work because it would mean more time away from the family. That sort of value system is unheard of in the broadcast newsrooms of New York, where furthering your career is assumed to be the name of the game. But this reporter's family salutes a different flag. The choice to turn away more assignments is not easy, but it's not hard either, because of a fundamental choice they have made about their family. They base that choice on their core beliefs about the meaning and value of what they have together.

Of course, a different couple faced with identical circumstances might do things differently. That's fine. Spirituality is less about following a set of dos and don'ts than about cultivating a deeper sense of purpose and conviction that is evidenced by a moral lifestyle. This is a subtle but important point. We can't comment on how people from other religious traditions wrestle with this principle, but as Christians, we're aware that people of our persuasion have a terrible reputation for mistaking rigid morality for spiritual vitality. As if life consisted of getting a perfect score on an exam!

Make no mistake: We believe in standards and moral absolutes. But these have an empty ring to them when they form the sum of a person's (or a couple's) spiritual life. We've seen marriages in which everything is tightly scripted according to black-and-white categories. He has his role, and she has hers; the boundaries are set in concrete. Expectations are precisely defined; deviations are unacceptable. In short, the couples are doing their relationships "by the book." The question is, Are they *alive?* Is there joy in their marriages? Is there any possibility for the unpredictable—where most of life has to be lived? The inner life, anyway.

Cultivating that inner life—that inner core—is not easy. But it's not impossible either. In a moment we'll offer a few suggestions of our own for doing that. But first some comments about a rather strange notion—the idea that business travel both affects and is affected by a couple's spirituality.

A Spirituality of Travel?

Of all the areas of marriage we've discussed, the spiritual dimension of the marriage relationship would seem to be the least affected by business travel. If a traveler runs off and doesn't call home for days at a time, that's going to seriously affect things at home. If a traveler's finances go to pieces because they get neglected while he or she is on the road, that's going to be felt very quickly. But what difference does going on the road make as to whether the marriage sustains its spiritual core?

Three thoughts come to mind.

1. Spirituality Nurtures the Marriage

Spirituality both nurtures and is nurtured by every other area of a marriage relationship. In this book, we have considered ten of these areas: commitment and trust, communication, conflict, loneliness, sexual intimacy and romance, parenting, finances, planning and scheduling, saying good-bye, and re-entry. Stop and think for a moment about the spiritual implications of these areas for your own marriage.

For example, take a phone call from the road. A phone call is a simple thing, really. Unremarkable. Travelers phone home all the time. Yet what is the meaning of a call? Beyond the *content* of what is said, there is a lot more going on—or should be. As we saw in chapter 2, a phone call forms a connection between two spouses. It says, "We're still here for each other. We need each other. We want to stay in touch. This relationship matters to us. We value it. We value each other. We value ourselves enough to keep this relationship alive." A simple phone call can mean that and a whole

190

lot more. Thus, the call can help to preserve and cultivate a spiritual connection.

But a call is also influenced by whatever spiritual foundation already exists. After all, spirituality affects behavior and attitudes. It helps determine whether you are caring and kind and patient and loving, or selfish and inconsiderate and impatient and cold. So when the spiritual foundation is solid, a phone call from the road can instantly renew the marriage bond. But if the foundation is weak, a call can put distance in the relationship; it may even contribute to tearing it down.

For example, let's listen in on a call placed from a pay phone at a busy airport (obviously, we can hear only one side of the conversation): "Hey! . . . Yeah, I'm between flights. . . . Five-thirty. . . . Yeah. . . . Yeah? . . . Really! . . . I guess so. . . . Yeah. . . . That's great, honey! . . . Yeah, me too. . . . Okay, bye!"

Judging by these rather terse responses, you would hardly think that anything of a spiritual nature is taking place. Just your basic phone call from the road, right? Maybe and maybe not. A lot depends on the quality of the couple's spiritual relationship. If it has little vitality, this phone call may be a lifeless, almost meaningless exercise. Indeed, it may be a chore.

However, let's say this couple enjoys a deep understanding of each other, coming from years of intimate conversations, shared experiences, honest arguments, apologies, forgiveness, and a mutual agreement on what matters most in life. In that case, a few one-word responses on the fly may be all it takes sometimes to communicate meaningfully. Thanks to a spiritual core that already exists, even the simple answer "yeah" to a question may be full of significance.

A similar relationship between spirituality and behavior could be drawn out for other aspects of marriage. The point is that spirituality is a factor in everything a couple does. So when travel affects any part of their relationship, it affects their spiritual life. Conversely, their spiritual life ends up affecting the way they deal with travel.

2. Spirituality Fosters Accountability

We looked at accountability earlier in discussing commitment (chapter 5). Accountability has to do with honoring our commit-

Good for Heart, Body, and Soul

We are hardly alone in believing religion can benefit your marriage and family life. For centuries, the Judeo-Christian tradition, along with other traditions, has honored the institution of marriage. More recently, scientific studies have corroborated the positive results of valuing and nurturing the family unit.

For example, Larry Larson and Mary Ann Mayo report that those who attend church, even if it's only once a month, increase their chances of staying married. Larson and Mayo believe this is because church attendance gives couples "a sense of shared values, ideology, and purpose in life. Christianity provides support for married couples to be committed, to show respect, to be emotionally supportive, to communicate effectively, and to create a stable power structure for the home. This intimacy solidifies the marriage romantically and sexually."

As to this last point, Larson and Mayo cite a number of studies indicating that religious observance can positively reinforce sexuality. "Most studies of marital adjustment are based on measures of satisfaction, perceived cohesion (how close and unified one feels with the other), and how free one feels to exchange feelings. A woman who goes to church regularly and who takes her religion seriously will report generally higher marital satisfaction regardless of whether sex is satisfying or not. Religious women were also the most satisfied with the frequency of intercourse and felt free to discuss sex openly with their husbands, and, most surprisingly, were more orgasmic than were the nonreligious" (Marianne K. Hering, "Believe Well, Live Well," *Focus on the Family,* September 1997, p. 4).

Other medical research has shown that religious people enjoy remarkable benefits to health, marriage, sexuality, and relationships in general. David Larson, a psychiatrist and medical

(continued)

192

researcher, spent ten years surveying data related to religion and good health, during his tenure at the National Institutes of Health. In 1992, he published a report in *The American Journal of Psychiatry* in which he summarized twelve years of psychiatric literature.

Larson found that when measuring religious commitment—defined as having a relationship with God and participating in religious ceremonies—"more than 90 percent of the studies supported the view that religion benefits mental health." According to Larson, the studies show that churchgoers have less heart disease, recover from burns and hip fractures faster, have lower blood pressure, and stay out of the hospital more often than those who don't worship.

Prayer especially has an impact on healing. In *The Power of Prayer and the Practice of Medicine,* Dr. Larry Dossey writes that "experiments with people showed that prayer positively affected high blood pressure, wounds, heart attacks, headaches, and anxiety."

In short, from preventing cataclysmic health problems, to minimizing chronic stress, to maximizing communication, to increasing sexual satisfaction, there seems to be wide agreement, both in the religious and the medical communities, that having a relationship with God and building your marriage on a strong spiritual foundation tend to benefit your life and relationships.

ment to our spouse, knowing that we will answer to him or her for everything we do. It's easy to see the importance of operating with a sense of accountability when a couple is separated by many miles. There are many distractions and temptations, both for the traveler on the road and for the spouse at home. Accountability acts as a conscience that helps protect their relationship.

Unfortunately, for many people the notion of accountability has a negative connotation. It feels confining and authoritarian. But accountability need not be oppressive. Again, a lot depends on the quality of the couple's spiritual foundation. We know of couples who are so in tune with one other that they remain connected in a spiritual sense no matter how far apart they may be. It's as if they carry each other in their hearts throughout the day, so in a given situation, they think and behave *as if* their loved one were standing right next to them. That's a beautiful thing to see! There's accountability, but it's joyful and empowering, not doleful or restrictive. It inspires the couple to deepen their love—even though they cannot do so in person. They do so in spirit instead.

3. Spirituality Brings God into the Marriage

Couples are accountable to each other, but they are accountable to God as well. This is often reflected in a couple's wedding ceremony, when the minister points out, "We are gathered *in the sight of God* and these witnesses." Likewise, the marriage vows begin with the declaration that they are being made "in the name of God." Statements like these affirm that God takes marriage seriously; therefore the couple will, as well. Their marriage will be a relationship not only between the two of them but between them and God.

Laying a Firm Foundation

The importance of building your marriage on a spiritual foundation cannot be overstated. Jim's role as a corporate chaplain often brings him in contact with couples who are struggling greatly in their marriages. Some of them are on the verge of divorce by the time they finally express a need for help. Invariably, Jim finds that, among the rest of their troubles, they have allowed the spiritual dimension of their relationship to slide.

That is so tragic because it is so needless. Any couple can take steps to deepen their spiritual roots. The more they do, the greater the likelihood that their marriage will stand strong in the day-to-day storms of life as well as when hit by gale-force winds.

We're not going to suggest any sort of easy formula to instant spirituality. Life doesn't work that way. But there are some basic principles and habits that have been universally acknowledged through the centuries as having value for your spiritual life. We encourage you and your spouse to incorporate these into your relationship in ways that make the most sense for you.

Mutually Decide Your Spiritual Life Is Important

It will be hard to build a spiritual foundation for your marriage if you and your spouse never discuss spiritual things. Somewhere along the way, you need to sit down and talk about what matters in life to both of you. That is, what *really* matters. What are you looking for out of life? What is your aim? What things are most important to you? What passions do you live for? What convictions are you willing to die for? What do you want to be remembered for when all is said and done? What do you consider sacred? Who or what do you serve as the highest power in the universe?

By exploring questions like these—and there are many more that could be asked—you and your spouse can begin to identify some of the bedrock elements on which you intend to build your relationship. Ideally, this discussion should be ongoing. Life is a journey, an odyssey, and your sense of meaning and purpose grows over time as you mature and gain more experience. So it's important to keep the dialogue going day by day in order to grow deeper with each other.

However, one decision that you as a couple ought to make at a definite moment in time is the choice to cultivate your spiritual lives. This is really a commitment to a way of life. It's a commitment to avoid living superficially and aimlessly. You may not always live up to that ideal, but at least you've both acknowledged that your life together is a treasure, a gift to be unwrapped. That puts you in a frame of mind to keep seeking the highest values and the greater meaning for yourselves.

By the way, we realize that for some people, "spirituality" sounds sort of abstract and esoteric. For that reason, they hesitate to even discuss it. "Look, I'm not interested in scraping the Milky Way with a lot of religious mumbo jumbo," some hard-boiled business types will say. "I like to keep my feet on the ground. I have no time for floating off into the ozone and getting all mystical!"

195

If that describes you, by all means keep your feet on the ground! You don't need to get mystical to have a lively center to your life or marriage. The most important thing is to be real and honest. At the same time, be open to the fact that everyone is different and therefore has a different spiritual experience.

Cultivate the Habit of Prayer

Prayer may be the oldest of all the spiritual disciplines. It is a habit that a majority of Americans say they practice privately, yet it's doubtful that very many couples practice it together. That's too bad, because in our experience, one of the best ways to develop intimacy with another person is to pray with him or her.

Without dwelling on the religious dimensions of prayer, here are three practical suggestions.

1. Pray Together

Some couples have never prayed together and feel a bit threatened by the whole idea of doing so. One way to break the ice is by

A Tried and True Foundation

Couples have good reason to pursue a traditional understanding of marriage. One researcher has discovered that 80 percent of couples who live together before marriage get divorced. Interestingly, he also finds that 60 percent of couples married by a justice of the peace ultimately divorce, as opposed to 40 percent of couples married in a church (the assumption being that those married in a religious setting rather than a secular or civil setting are more likely to be tying their marriage to their religious commitment).

By the way, only 1 out of 1,051 people who read and study the Bible regularly get divorced! Thus, it would appear that concrete religious beliefs and behaviors add a significant success factor to marriages.

establishing a routine of briefly praying before meals. At the very least, you can express thanks for the food. If you feel up to it, you can also pray about any needs that are current in the family—a child's health, a relative's need for a job, safe travel during an upcoming trip. Mealtimes are a natural occasion at which to pause for a moment and join together in a simple prayer. The words need not be profound—just sincere.

2. Pray Silently

We are willing to bet that in the majority of marriages today, couples do not pray together because they are afraid to pray out loud in front of each other. Who knows why that may be the case? One reason is probably because prayer can be very revealing. In any case, if being afraid to pray out loud is a reason why you and your spouse do not pray together, we suggest that you pray together *silently.* Prayers don't have to be spoken out loud to be heard (at least, they don't in the Judeo-Christian tradition). Again, the words are not nearly so important as the *fact* that you pray and that you pray *together.*

3. Pray before, during, and after Trips

Consider the possibility of using business trips as a natural time to engage in prayer.

> *Before the trip:* a prayer for safety, both on the road and at home, for a productive trip, for encouragement, for strength
> *During the trip:* prayers for loved ones far away
> *After the trip:* a prayer of thanksgiving for a safe journey, and a prayer to celebrate the reunion

Try this regimen a few times. You may be amazed at the different attitude it creates about those nasty trips that prove so intrusive to family life!

Read Uplifting Writings

Read, meditate on, and discuss writings that uplift the spirit and honor the institution of marriage. For Christians and Jews,

197

the Bible is a natural choice in this regard. There's a reason why it remains the best-selling book in the world. Its literary value alone makes it worthwhile. But its greatest use to you is that it's a timeless source of wisdom.

Other helpful material can be found in poetry, reflective essays, biographies, and journals—for example, the sonnets of John Milton or William Shakespeare, Mike Mason's *The Mystery of Marriage*, cited earlier, or some of C. S. Lewis's writings on marriage. The point is to allow the wisdom of the ages to inform your spiritual perspective. If you will feed your mind on these thoughts and discuss them with your spouse, you will find that they can strengthen your relationship. They will help you sort out what you genuinely believe, what is true about life, and what is worth holding on to. They will also lead you into areas that otherwise you might never explore.

Find Others Who Share Your Beliefs

Get together with others who are like-minded in terms of values and beliefs. This is the value of community. It goes without saying that modern society tends to hinder the sense of community for most of us. Thus, we have to be intentional and proactive in cultivating significant relationships.

By *community*, we're not thinking so much of acquaintances at work and neighbors next door, important as those relationships are. Rather, we have in mind a handful of other couples who share your understanding of life and with whom you can talk about spiritual matters. You need not agree on everything; indeed, you'll benefit from people who challenge your perspectives and offer insights of their own. But you need a group of friends who will affirm your deepest beliefs and support you as you work out the implications of those beliefs for your marriage.

One thing to consider is going back to church, perhaps the church of your youth. Or if that proved dissatisfying in the past, ask a coworker about his or her church, or even look up a congregation in the phone book or the religious section of the newspaper. Or consider some kind of Bible study or support group that meets in the workplace.

Develop Family Traditions to Reinforce Spirituality

One reason why religions prove so enduring and powerful is that they formalize spiritual commitment. They provide rituals and symbols that translate abstract beliefs into concrete terms that everyday folk can understand. When adherents participate in these symbolic activities, their connection to the faith is reinforced and deepened.

You can apply this same principle to the spiritual life of your home by introducing traditions that grow out of your spiritual foundation. For example, a moment ago we mentioned prayer before meals. This is a simple exercise, but it can be profoundly valuable as a ritual of faith. The *act* of praying can communicate a number of things to everyone in your family: that you believe in God (if you are praying to God); that you recognize God's hand in the provision of your material needs; that your family is a unit (shown by praying *together*); that you believe your family's spiritual life is important; that you act on your beliefs.

There are many other ways to formally express your spirituality. One family developed the tradition of taking a family portrait each year during the holidays. Another made a habit of participating in a Veterans Day parade, as a number of the family's forebears had fought and died for freedom. One couple made a point of repeating their marriage vows to each other every year on their anniversary. Another pair made a return visit to the park where they had first met, whenever they had a major problem or decision to discuss.

Use your creativity to devise and plan traditions that have meaning for you. And think small and simple, not just big and fancy. That is, allow for rituals that fit into the warp and woof of daily life, as well as rituals that occur on special occasions. Anyone can get emotionally charged up for a parade or a special meal. But it's when we celebrate our spiritual values in the day-to-day routines of life that we show they are genuine.

By the way, traditions that reinforce spirituality are especially helpful in light of business travel. Obviously, travel means separation. And if travelers and their families are not careful, physical separation can quickly translate into spiritual estrangement

Back on Solid Ground

As the corporate chaplain at Interstate, Jim has often seen seemingly doomed marriages turn around and succeed when the couple gives attention to their spiritual lives. For example, Jim recently asked one of the Interstate salesmen, whom we'll call Art, how he and his wife were doing.

Two years before, Art had come to Jim for help with some serious trouble he and his wife were having. Married for thirteen years, they were experiencing less and less intimacy and more and more conflict, with less ability to identify areas of common interest. It seemed as if their relationship was headed in two different directions—and downhill fast!

The interesting thing was that Art had grown up in a deeply religious home, where principles of building life on a strong spiritual foundation had been taught. But over the years, he had become indifferent to those values and developed a habit of ignoring them in his own family life. However, in the few brief sessions he had with Jim, Jim urged him to reconsider the beliefs his parents had tried to instill in him.

Jim couldn't tell whether Art would take that advice or what the outcome of his marriage would be. So it was as much out of curiosity as concern that Jim asked Art one day how things were going.

"Unbelievable!" Art replied, much to Jim's pleasant surprise. Jim asked Art to explain. He learned that after their conversations, Art had made up his mind to return to his spiritual roots. As Art put it, he had sought and failed to find meaning, direction, and purpose apart from God. Maybe it was time he returned to God. So he began attending church again, ostensibly for the sake of his children. To his surprise, however, he found it beneficial for himself. And also to his surprise, his wife did not oppose this new

(continued)

activity, even though Art had expected a retaliatory, negative response. Indeed, she eventually started attending church, as well—slowly at first but with no prodding from Art.

The long-term result was a dramatic, "unbelievable" turnaround in the couple's marriage. Art explained that they now have a common source of strength for accepting and dealing with their weaknesses, a source of guidance for their decisions, a peace in the midst of their anxieties, solutions for their frustrations, and a new love in their marriage as a result of their newfound relationship with God.

Jim was overjoyed with this report. But the truth is, he has seen that kind of outcome time and again when couples build their lives and marriages on a strong spiritual foundation.

as well. But traditions help counteract that. They can create a powerful bond between the traveler and those at home. They serve as important events to anticipate and prepare for and as memorable events to look back on with fondness and insight. These experiences of anticipation and memory form subtle but powerful ties.

An Explanation—and an Invitation

Our aim in writing this book has been to be practical and realistic. To some, this would seem to rule out what we have called the spiritual side of life. Yet because marriage and family life ultimately are based on these core beliefs and values, it would be highly *un*realistic for us to ignore the spiritual dimension.

However, in speaking about this issue, we're aware that for some readers, thinking along these lines may feel strange and unfamiliar. Or it may recall a yearning of the soul that they have been trying to satisfy for many years, without success. We've indicated that we have based our lives and marriages on Jesus Christ. What does that mean?

Jesus said that he had come so that people might have life in all of its fullness. He was promising a life that is more than just rushing around in busyness, or beating our heads against the wall in day-to-day routine. He was saying that because of him, we can *really live!*

In today's cynical society, that may sound like a stretch. But the fact is that God really does care about our lives. God is even aware of the travails and tensions posed by everyday things like business travel. He knows about them because Jesus, as the God-man, lived a busy life on this planet for some thirty-three years. It was through Jesus' life, and ultimately through his death, that God reconnected with humanity.

We say *reconnect* because we human beings are estranged from God. We all experience that spiritual disconnection from time to time, and it goes back to a root problem that both the Old and New Testaments of the Bible call sin. Sin involves a separation in our relationship with God, the One who made us. And apart from God, there is death, not "life in all of its fullness."

So it was to bridge this gaping disconnection that Jesus came. He freely laid down his life—not to provide a moral standard or to be a martyr or to start a new religion but to reunite us with God and give us life in all of its fullness.

That, at any rate, is the claim of the New Testament. Both of us believe that claim, and we have found new life and meaning as a result. Naturally, we recommend the same for you. In fact, if you do not know God, we invite you to re-establish that relationship, just as we have. It involves an act of faith: acknowledging that you too are estranged from God, and trusting Jesus' death and resurrection to bridge the gap and restore your relationship with God.

Perhaps the most common way of expressing that initial faith is in a prayer, in which you affirm those things to God. Using your own words, you can admit your personal sin and your need for Jesus' payment for that sin. You can express trust in Jesus' death to have made that payment and tell God you are willing to re-establish a relationship. You can pray that prayer whenever you're ready, wherever you are. In fact, why not do so right now?

Of course, you may have questions or need more information before taking that step. You may not even be sure whether what we're saying is true, but you're curious to find out more. If so, feel free to contact us at Front Line Outreach, 12770 Merit Drive, Suite 400, Dallas, TX 75251. We'll be glad to reply or put you in touch with someone in your area who can help.

Obviously, we take our faith pretty seriously. It's not because we're perfect but because we're human. Jesus brings stability and balance to our lives and our marriages in an oftentimes chaotic and certainly less-than-perfect world. We're convinced that a spiritual foundation is the key to a significant life and family. Jesus put it this way: "Therefore everyone who hears these words of Mine, and acts upon them, may be compared to a wise man, who built his house upon the rock. And the rain descended, and the floods came, and the winds blew, and burst against that house; and yet it did not fall, for it had been founded upon the rock. And everyone who hears these words of Mine, and does not act upon them, will be like a foolish man, who built his house upon the sand. And the rain descended, and the floods came, and the winds blew, and burst against that house; and it fell, and great was its fall" (Matt. 7:24–27).

Two approaches to life. Two foundations. Two outcomes. The choice is ours.

Is Your Company's Travel Policy Family-Friendly?

More and more companies are recognizing the vital connection between work and family life. How does your company stack up on the issue of business travel? Use the inventory below to evaluate your organization's travel policy and programs.

1. We evaluate the frequency and duration of our employees' trips and take steps, when necessary, to prevent overload.
2. We have a hot line or other means by which spouses and family members can contact us about travel-related problems.
3. We have an 800 number that travelers can use for help in dealing with family-related matters from the road.
4. We discourage Saturday night stayovers solely to cut air fare costs for the company.
5. We offer to pay for at least one long-distance phone call home each day.
6. We allow employees to keep their frequent flyer mileage.
7. We provide a "concierge" service to assist employees with managing their personal affairs while they are out of town.
8. We offer child and/or elderly parent care or reimbursement for such care during a traveler's absence.
9. When a work assignment requires an extended stay out of town (several weeks or months), we offer to fly workers home on weekends to be with their families.
10. We allow travelers who have been on the road for an extended period (four or more days) to take a day or even two days off upon their return to be with their families.
11. We formally brief travelers on how travel may affect their families.
12. We provide counseling services for couples and families who request it.

13. We consider employees' requests for the timing of business trips and, under some circumstances, allow them veto power over when a trip is scheduled.
14. We have a formal program to address the issues raised by the effect of travel on marriage and family life.

If your company would like to develop a family-friendly travel policy and minimize the impact of business travel on employees and their families, contact Bill Hendricks or Jim Coté at Front Line Outreach, 12770 Merit Drive, Suite 400, Dallas, TX 75251.

William Hendricks, who holds degrees from Harvard, Boston University, and Dallas Theological Seminary, is the author or coauthor of twelve books and is president of the Hendricks Group, a communications consulting firm in Dallas, Texas. He and his wife, Nancy, have three daughters.

Jim Coté, who holds a business degree from LeTourneau University, is corporate chaplain for Interstate Batteries and is director of Interstate's Marriage and the Road program. He and his wife, Brenda, have three sons.